PEOPLES OF ROMAN BRITAIN

General Editor Keith Branigan
Professor of Prehistory and Archaeology
University of Sheffield

PARISI

CORNOVII

CORITANI

ICENI

TRINOVANTES

SILURES

DOBUNNI

CATUVELLAUNI

ATREBATES

BELGAE

CANTIACI

REGNI

DUROTRIGES

DUMNONII

0   50
⊢ ⊣ ⊣ ⊣ ⊣ ⊣ miles

THE
PARISI

HERMAN RAMM
Investigator, Royal Commission on
Historical Monuments

DUCKWORTH

First published in 1978 by
Gerald Duckworth & Co. Ltd.
The Old Piano Factory
43 Gloucestor Crescent,
London, NW1

Cased ISBN 0 7156 1167 4

Paper ISBN 0 7156 1168 2

To Mrs Mary Chitty, who as Mary Kitson Clark produced the pioneer book upon which all subsequent work on the Romans in East Yorkshire is based.

Photoset by
Specialised Offset Services Ltd., Liverpool
and printed by
Unwin Brothers Ltd, Old Woking

Contents

Acknowledgments

I wish to thank the secretary of the Royal Commission on Historical Monuments for giving me permission to use material based on fieldwork and interpretation of air photographs by myself and my colleagues on the staff of the Commission. Any opinions and inferences are, however, my own and do not necessarily reflect those of the commissioners. I would like to thank my colleagues and others who have allowed me to use unpublished material or discussed individual points with me, in particular Ian Stead, Ray Farrar, Ron Butler, Ian Goodall, Vivien Swan, Chris Dunn, Stephen Johnson, Brian Hartley, John Dent, Rod Mackey and Peter Wenham. Without their help and that of numerous others, past and present, this book would have been impossible to write. Every archaeologist in East Yorkshire owes a debt of gratitude to those who carry out aerial reconnaissance, in particular to Dr St. Joseph, John Hampton, David Wilson, Tony Paccito, Derrick Riley and Tony Brewster.

Archaeologists who work in East Yorkshire have to rely on the results of aerial reconnaisance probably more heavily than in any other area. Interpretation of air photographs must always be subjective and interim, and readers of this book must bear this in mind. All surveys based on archaeological evidence must be incomplete, even more so where that evidence is mainly that of air photographs of crop-marks. The Parisi rarely appear in history, and their very existence as an organised *civitas* has been disputed. Compression in a book of this kind will make many statements appear as dogmatic fact which are essentially hypothetical. The author can only attempt to provide a framework which will be of use to future workers, but one which is itself very vulnerable to new discoveries. The latest air photographs consulted were flown in 1974.

Illustrations

Line Drawings by Jennifer Gill

1. Tribal Territory and the Pre-Roman Iron Age

East Yorkshire is dominated by the Wolds (fig. 1), an area of chalk downland, now mainly under the plough, which reaches in places to a height of over 240 metres. To the south the Humber flows through a gap in a narrow ridge with a marked western escarpment which continues north for 36 km. almost to Malton before turning east. The gentler eastern slopes extend in a crescentic curve north-east and then east to end in the bold chalk cliffs of Flamborough. To the south-east, within the crescent, is the low-lying but hummocky plain of Holderness. The Vales of York and Pickering lie respectively west and north of the Wolds, separated by the Howardian Hills, a north-western extension of the narrow Jurassic band that flanks and forms a lower step to the western escarpment of the Wolds. The northern edge of the Vale of Pickering is a broken limestone escarpment, declining gradually to the Vale and deeply incised by gorges. This southern fringe of the North Yorkshire Moors, separated by valleys and cliffs from the wilder areas and poorer soils of the Moors proper, belongs naturally to our area, as also do the sands of the eastern side of the Vale of York as far west as the Derwent. Thus there are two upland zones, the chalk of the Wolds, and the limestone of the Howardian Hills and the northern fringe of the Vale of Pickering, and three low-lying areas, the Vale of Pickering, the eastern edge of the Vale of York, and the plain of Holderness. The low-lying areas are far from uniform. In Holderness the Hull valley runs south from Driffield to the Humber and is floored with peaty deposits locally known as carrs, areas of marshy ground which give way to marine silts between

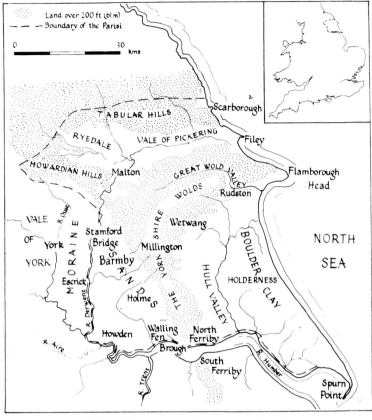

1.   Map of the area showing the natural regions

Beverley and Hull. These expanses of carr and silt lands are
interrupted by patches of boulder clay, sand and gravel
forming knolls and islands of higher ground on which are now
sited the older villages and farms. This irregular relief of 3 to 9
metres rises towards the coast, which is followed by a ridge of
undulating glacial deposits 15 to 30 metres above sea level and
terminating seawards in a long low unindented line of boulder
clay cliffs. The Vale of Pickering, broad and flat-bottomed at
some eighteen metres above sea level, has its full share of
marshy carr lands, its inheritance from a former large glacial
lake, but amongst these are many islands of well-drained

sands and gravels and the Vale is flanked by glacial deposits and sealed from the coast by a morainic ridge. The river Derwent, which drains the Vale of Pickering, after passing through the limestone hills in a gorge, follows the eastern side of the Vale of York and only joins the Ouse west of Howden. To the south-east of the Vale of York, where the land rarely rises above 3 metres, are areas of former swamp such as Walling Fen, but north of this fenland there are, east of the Derwent, large areas of sand.

The Wolds now form an almost treeless, windswept chalk plateau intersected by deep waterless valleys. Streams rarely occur and where they do may be intermittent, fed by springs locally known as 'gypseys', a name popularly believed to have arisen from the vagrancy of the water, but in fact applied to these springs before the vagrants were so-called. One larger valley, the Great Wold Valley, which cuts right across the downland, contains a stream and because of the presence of water has always been a focus for settlement. A line of modern villages with any gaps filled by the earthworks of deserted mediaeval settlement is set amongst the almost continuous crop-marks of still earlier periods. Water must always have been a problem on the chalk. Mediaeval villages were usually sited where it was possible to have meres retaining a store, one for men and one for beasts, and shallow wells. The Romans also relied on wells, although there is one example of an aqueduct. Earlier, since wells are not found, people must have relied on surface collection, possibly in a similar way to the dew-ponds of the late eighteenth century after the discovery of an effective method of lining them that was not easily pierced.[1]

Water, in short supply on the Wolds, could be too plentiful elsewhere. The Vale of York, watered rather than drained by its rivers, and the valley of the Hull, another sluggish stream, have been subject to extensive flooding down to recent times and may well be again. But flooding has varied in frequency from period to period as well as in extent. One period when flooding and consequent waterlogging affected settlement is the later end of the fourth century and into the fifth and sixth,[2] another is the pre-Roman iron age.[3]

The map, fig. 2, shows the extent of the 1625 floods[4] in the Vale of York. Marine transgression both before and after the

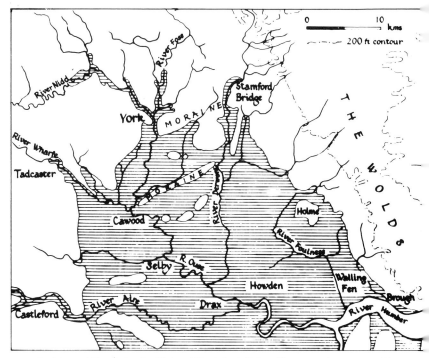

2. Map of floods in the Vale of York in 1625 to illustrate the extent of late Roman and early post-Roman flooding

Roman period and consequent ponding behind the barrier of the Wolds must have caused similar but more frequent floods which would have waterlogged most of the Vale south of York and rendered it inhospitable to settlement. The Hull valley was also vulnerable and, although there would not be the same ponding here, waterlogging took place some distance up the drainage system, where local topography caused poor drainage, as Varley[5] has shown.

Comparison of the extent of the 1625 floods with the distribution of square-ditched barrows (fig. 4) implies that resettlement of some areas had begun before the Roman conquest, and that Stead's[6] suggestion that the Romans found the Vale of York sparsely populated requires qualification. Nevertheless it is true in general terms that Roman settlement was heavier than that in the Iron Age except on the moraines and eastern fringes. The history of the site of the possible *civitas* capital at Brough illustrates the changing environmental conditions. The pre-Roman crossing of the Humber was between North and South Ferriby where the 7.6 metre contour is cut by the shore line. The Roman crossing between Winteringham and Brough, where the shore is at 3 metres, possessed in the shingled bottom of the haven at Brough, clear advantages which were not useable in the previous period of frequent flood. Its vulnerability was demonstrated at the end of the Roman period when the site again lost its advantages and dwindled to unimportance during the later fourth century.[7]

In addition to such major marine transgressions resulting from fluctuations in the height of sea-level, the boulder clay coast south of Flamborough has been subjected to steady erosion, now eating into the land at the rate of 1.5 to 2 metres a year and demonstrated vividly by a comparison of the first edition six-inch ordnance maps surveyed in 1851-2 with those of most recent date. The material eroded is redeposited on the north side of the Humber estuary and contributes to the periodic reformation of Spurn Point. The coast of today must differ in many ways from the Roman. A strip at least a mile wide has been eroded since A.D. 600, together with numerous important mediaeval settlements, including the port of Ravenser Odd where Henry IV landed in 1399.[8] That Roman sites have also been lost is demonstrated by the finds frequently made in the crumbling cliffs.

If the waterlogged vale proved a barrier to traffic, it should be emphasised that rivers as such did not, and indeed the reverse was probably the case, and the dendritic river system leading into the Humber provided lines of penetration far inland. The Humber estuary was a door open towards the continent, and the navigable Ouse provided a back entry into our area, as the use made of it by Harald Hardrada in 1066 on his way to the battle of Stamford Bridge[9] clearly illustrates. Rivers were often fordable. A natural ford across the Derwent at Stamford Bridge[10] lay at the east end of the York and Escrick moraines, two ridges across the Vale of York which provided a natural trackway well known in the archaeological literature. Even without severe waterlogging the York moraine retained its importance throughout the Roman period, as the siting of York and the road system illustrates.

The environmental conditions described continued to affect settlement and land use long after the period discussed in this book. This later land use, as well as factors more directly related to the natural regions, has affected both the survival and recognition of archaeological features. An obvious example of the effect of differing soils on recognition of sites, with a consequent distortion of distribution maps, is the ability of chalk to develop crop-marks, whilst boulder clays are a poor medium. Waterlogging may result in the growth of peat over a site, flooding may hide it below an alluvial deposit and in neither case will there be crop-marks. A combination of human and natural factors can subtly affect survival. For example, where the floor of Garton Slack narrows into Wetwang Slack, the removal of a protective plantation accompanied by ploughing of the valley slope has led to the run-off of water depositing a thin layer of marl which is sufficient to mask crop-marks readily visible on the wider valley floor to the east. To understand the distribution of early sites it is essential to know the later history of land use in any area.

On the Wolds the territory of the mediaeval village was divided between arable and pasture. Many factors, including a growth in monastic ownership, led to a gradual reduction in arable and encroachment of pasture and the consequent desertion of some of the villages. This process reached its peak in the eighteenth century when a great part of the Wolds had been turned to sheep-walks.[11] This trend was reversed by the agricultural revolution. The enclosures of open fields and commons which in this area generally happened between 1770 and 1830, the demand for corn that resulted from the Revolutionary and Napoleonic wars, combined with the advantages offered by the Corn Laws and the work of improving landlords such as Sir Christopher Sykes who 'transformed [the country about Sledmere] from an open, sandy, barren, extensive sheep walk ... into well cultivated farms, adorned with plantations',[12] led gradually to the present position where most of the Wolds are arable and very little of the old pasture is left except on the sides of the deep valleys. The result of this history is that in each parish three zones can be observed; the village, the area of old arable sometimes visible as ridge and furrow, and further out the old pasture which may never have been ploughed until the nineteenth century. The village usually occupies the best settlement site in the area but except for chance finds or the opportunity provided by redevelopment, or by excavation of a deserted mediaeval village, seldom reveals the evidence for its earliest occupation. The area of old pasture is, in its present cultivation, very amenable to air-photography, and in the nineteenth century was subject to the observations of antiquaries such as the Mortimers and Greenwell. But it must be remembered that ploughing was already well under way when they were working, and that the Mortimers for example were only interested in barrows and dikes. J.R. Mortimer dismisses the hill-fort at Grimthorpe casually with a reference to the 'filled up inner ditch of a supposed camp'.[13] The intermediate zone of the old arable varies in the crop-marks it will show. Ridge and furrow, extant or only recently ploughed, will obscure the remains below. Even where ploughed for a considerable time the greater depth of plough soil resulting from the levelling of the ridges will limit the appearance of crop-marks to the best conditions of crop and climate. The recently discovered Roman fort at Hayton was in a pasture field under extant ridge and furrow until some twenty years ago. In 1967 air photographs still showed only the crop-marks of ridge and furrow, and it was not until 1974 that the latter had been destroyed sufficiently to reveal the fort ditches.

In the low-lying areas additional factors came into play. Many of the sandy moors and commons must have had earthworks surviving but unrecorded as late as on the Wolds, but except for sites on Skipwith Common failed to attract antiquarian interest and are now known only from air-photography. Sand and gravel show crop-marks well but the boulder clay, often as suitable for settlement, does not. Peat and alluvial deposits, whether natural or the result of warping, will cover other sites, and modern drainage will obscure the sites of the meres and lakes of larger or smaller extent which were once such a feature of Holderness and an important part of the Roman and pre-Roman landscape, and which must have affected the siting and nature of settlement.

Much of our new knowledge of the Parisi derives from air-photography. Even where, as on the Wolds, photographs taken over a period of twenty-five years can be studied and variations in annual climate and crop discounted, variations due not to archaeological distribution but differences of soil and subsequent land-use must be taken into account, as well as the subjectivity of much interpretation. Distribution patterns based on chance finds or the field work of previous investigators[14] may to some extent act as a corrective, but they are subject to other irrelevant factors such as the interests of the investigator, the accessibility of sites, and the presence of revealing agents such as building development, ploughing, and drainage.

Early settlement

The earliest known occupants of East Yorkshire are the mesolithic campers at Star Carr in the eighth millennium B.C. But these early wanderers, scattered and numerically insignificant, following the movement of game, or the availability of fish and wild fruits, settling only temporarily or in seasonal camps, cannot have had any great or lasting effect on the landscape. The first farmers were neolithic and here C14 dating shows that East Yorkshire belongs to the area of primary settlement. In spite of the painstaking work by Manby,[15] details of farms and fields are hard to come by, and the principal monuments and evidence for their distribution must remain the long barrow. This distribution concentrates on the Wolds and the Limestone, extending north from our area into the North Yorkshire Moors and south into Lincolnshire – the areas in which *prima facie* one would expect the first settlement, where light soils make clearance of scrub or woodland easier whether for grain cultivation or stock grazing. The evidence of the burial mounds is supported by the scanty occupation debris.

Turner[16] has suggested that the chalk Wolds were disforested by the mid-second millennium B.C. The weight of the distribution of the bronze age round barrows is similar to that of the long barrows, but from the beaker period onwards there is increasing evidence from the lower-lying areas. Beakers come from Staxton on the gravel shelf bordering the Vale of Pickering, and round barrows or ring ditches occur also on the sands and gravels of Holderness or the morainic ridges in the Vale of York. Dunn[17] has recently discussed the valley situation of ring ditches, and it should be noted that one of the ring ditches on the gravel terrace of the Derwent that occasioned his paper, contains an internal feature which almost exactly matches in plan that round the beaker grave in a barrow excavated by Brewster in Wetwang Slack.[18] The distribution is less concentrated in these areas not necessarily because it reflects a smaller original number, but because of factors operating against survival and recognition.

Settlement sites from the early to middle bronze age are rarely found. The barrows are easily identified and remained features in the landscape and were reused by later peoples for reburials or landmarks on which to lay out their dikes and fields, or to incorporate in a bank. Other less easily identified features probably also survive incapsulated in later patterns. Three or possibly four cursuses of late neolithic date centred on Rudston at the bend in the Great Wold Valley survived and were incorporated in later features – dikes, field boundaries, settlement enclosures – whose lay-out was dictated by their existence.

Late bronze and early iron age

In the late bronze age there is a change in the type of evidence. Barrows and burials no longer predominate in the archaeological record, and it has indeed been suggested that barrow building ceased in our area during this period. At Catfoss in Holderness[19] a flat cremation cemetery with bucket urns in pits within and around a circular penannular ditched enclosure may be paralleled by many others unrecognised among the many ring ditches visible on air photographs. Cremation burials on Ampleforth Common[20] in the Howardian Hills were in round barrows. Dated by C14 to *c.* 790 B.C. (after calibration), they probably reflect the local late bronze age tradition. Several barrows excavated by Mortimer on the Wolds contained unaccompanied cremations as primary or secondary burials and although without dating evidence these too are possibly late bronze age.

Finds of metalwork – swords, spearheads, socketed axes – either individually or in hoards, show a much wider distribution than earlier bronze age finds, including a marked concentration in Holderness. But much of this late bronze age equipment continued into the iron age, and sites as late as Staple Howe (C14 date after calibration, 750-520 B.C.) or Scarborough produce, in addition to metalwork showing Hallstatt influence and fragments of iron, much that reflects late bronze age tradition.

Open settlements are known from Holderness. At Ulrome and Barmston[21] the so-called Lake Villages produced areas of cobbling associated with hearths and the collapsed remains of wooden huts. Varley considers that the settlement at Barmston consisted of a hamlet of several rectangular huts in a fen hollow. These structures were found below a layer of peat indicating that the settlement was deserted as a result of periodic flooding. It was dated by C14 (calibrated) to *c.* 1200 B.C. Later settlement in the same area is indicated by square-ditched barrows on air photographs, presumably when conditions had again become less wet. Other sites have been found by chance, as at Burton Fleming and Octon Cross Roads, but on the whole the evidence is very slight.

A box-ramparted hill-fort such as that at Grimthorpe[22] on the west escarpment of the Wolds can more readily be accepted now as late bronze age than when the C14 dates were first published for the site. These give a date after calibration of *c.* 1220 B.C. for the construction of the fort, and of *c.* 870 B.C. for midden material from the ditch, which is comparable with the evidence for Dinorben and Ivinghoe. But there are still problems, since although some of the pottery forms will fit such an early date others 'argue an extended occupation into at least the later seventh century'.[23] The excavator did not, however, find evidence in the structures or elsewhere that implied a long period of occupation. A second but smaller fort, like Grimthorpe circular in plan and defended by a box rampart, has been excavated at Thwing[24] on the east side of the Wolds, producing undecorated bucket pottery. Other sites can be recognised from the air; five are circular or oval in plan but the sixth and largest, at Greenlands, Rudston, is more irregular.[25] Grimthorpe and Dearsden are on the west edge of the Wolds but the other six form a compact group on the eastern Wolds near Bridlington.

The picture is one of more widely distributed settlement over the whole of the area at the end of the bronze age. The expansion of population this implied was probably responsible for the strains within society that produced the hill-forts in the primary area of settlement on the chalk. In the seventh century Hallstatt C influence appears on sites around the Vale of Pickering both in the metalwork and the pottery. But the evidence from both Staple Howe and Scarborough is that much of the earlier traditions of the bronze age continued, and that the new influence is due to trade or the arrival of groups readily absorbed into the local population. The inhabitants at the key site of Staple Howe[26] were concerned enough about defence to choose an isolated knoll but preferred to defend themselves with a simple stockade rather than the box-rampart of Thwing or Grimthorpe. Scarborough[27] was a much larger type of settlement, and the concentration of thirty pits originally intended for storage but full of domestic rubbish could imply the zoning for different purposes often found within hill-forts. The mediaeval ramparts of the castle may well conceal some form of iron-age defence.

The distribution of Hallstatt metalwork, and of pottery showing Hallstatt influence, scattered and casual as the finds have been, is widespread across the whole of our area except for the Howardian Hills and south-eastern Holderness. Brewster was probably exaggerating when he suggested to Challis that there were over a hundred stockaded enclosures such as Staple Howe known in eastern Yorkshire, but there were certainly originally many more than the three of which Challis and Harding felt sure enough to put on their distribution map.[28] One such site, known from crop-marks, is the stockaded settlement south-west of Market Weighton (fig. 3), standing on a slightly elevated knoll indicated by the 50 ft. contour on the plan. Five round huts are visible concentrated

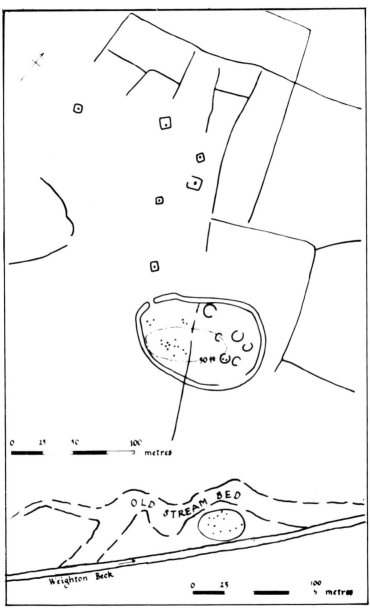

3. Plan of early iron age site on Weighton Common

into the east half of the enclosure. The site is overlaid by later enclosure ditches with associated square barrows, but it seems reasonable to associate two curvilinear enclosures as subsidiary to the stockaded settlement. At Thornham Hill[29] in north Holderness a ridge of glacial gravel rises above low-lying marshy ground. On it were seven round huts and considerable pottery. Four-poster structures, explained as granaries, were a feature both of Grimthorpe and Staple Howe. It is rare for a structure of this type to be visible on an air photograph, but one shows a rectangular hut at Burton Fleming associated with four-poster structures. At Garton Slack[30] Brewster has excavated a rectangular building as well as round huts. The latter, producing pottery of Staple Howe type, were scattered along the valley floor without apparent enclosure. Grimthorpe, Staple Howe and Scarborough all indicate that arable farming played an important part in the economy of the settlement. Examination of the food bones shows that ox, sheep, pig and horse were reared.

The Arras culture

Striking cultural changes took place in east Yorkshire from the mid-fifth century, of which the characteristic identifying feature is inhumation under a small barrow surrounded by a square ditch.[31] The culture is named from the rich cemetery at Arras near Market Weighton. Here a number of small barrows, from 2.5 to 8 metres across, of which some were certainly surrounded by ditches, square and not round in plan, covered burials including many without grave goods but three with 'chariots'. Estimates of the total number of barrows at Arras vary between 90 and 200. Several other large cemeteries of many hundreds of square barrows are now known by excavation or air photography from east Yorkshire and these include at least ten further 'chariot' burials. In addition to the large cemeteries, smaller ones of ten to twenty barrows are known as well an individual barrows and small groups. Within the barrows the usual burial is a contracted one within a central grave, although ditch and mound burials are also known and burials on the old land surface. With the burials there is often a joint of meat or a pot and occasionally a brooch, spearhead or sword. On occasion the corners of the squares are curved, and sometimes so curved as to be difficult to distinguish from ring ditches. At Eastburn[32] the burials were within ring ditches and at other places, such as Rillington, rings and squares are found together.[33]

The burials are not easily dated within the period, and although examples of relative chronology are available from Burton Fleming, Garton and Wetwang Slacks, we are not yet able to construct a chronological framework by which it would be possible to analyse the distribution shown on fig. 4 and to trace trends in the direction and growth of population. Stead dates Arras itself to the third or second century B.C. and sees the Danes Graves (fig. 5) and Eastburn cemeteries continuing in use almost to the Roman conquest. Challis and Harding, however have identified certain changes in emphasis in the immediate pre-Roman period.[34]

The geographical distribution can now be based on sufficient detail (fig. 4) to form at least a general idea of the distribution and weight of population within the area and the limits of the culture itself. Certain areas however have not been subjected to, or are not amenable to, the same study from air photography as the main part of the area. These include the northern limestone fringe of the Vale of Pickering where afforestation has taken place on a large scale. There are, however, a few sites recognised from old fieldwork and excavation – sufficient to indicate that there were probably many more. The Howardian Hills have not been subjected to much air photography and the absence of square barrows recorded in this area may not be significant. No barrows are so far known west of the river Ouse apart from one possible but doubtful crop-mark south of Tadcaster. Here Riley's sorties along the west side of the Vale of York do suggest that their absence is not accidental. Two other gaps along the lower Ouse and Derwent and in south-east Holderness should be noticed. The reason for the first is probably waterlogging during the period, but the second is harder to explain. Boulder clay is a poor agent for crop-marks, and this would explain the general thinning of the distribution in Holderness, but there are sufficient areas of sand and gravel to reveal the general continuance of the distribution and these areas exist also in the south-eastern part. Square barrows have not been recognised in the areas south of the Humber, but there are some possible examples from the Trent Valley.[35] The general thinness of the distribution on the chalk plateau should be noticed. The only area where the distribution has weight on the chalk is at Arras, where the Wolds are at their narrowest and are cut just to the north by valleys approaching from east

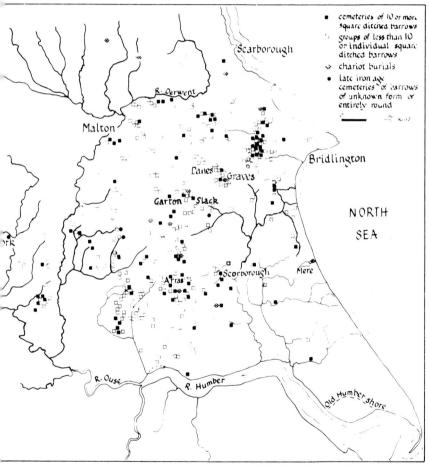

4. Distribution of iron age square ditched barrows

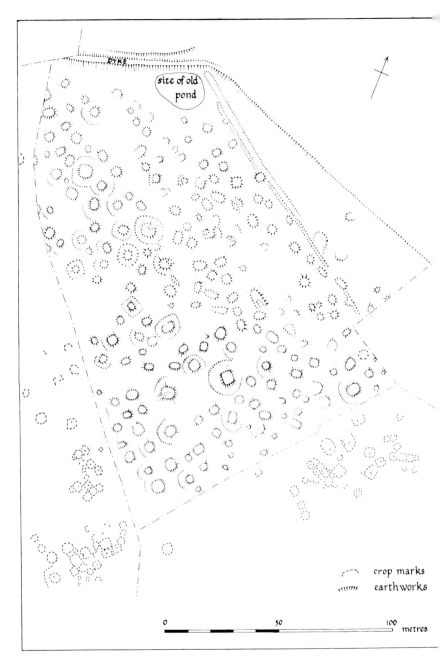

site of old pond

DYKE

- - - crop marks

⟿ earthworks

0   50   100 metres

5. Plan of iron age cemetery at Danes' Graves near Driffield

to west. The barrows are concentrated most heavily along the eastern fringe of the Wolds but with significant concentrations along the rivers Hull and Derwent and into the Vale of York. They extend as far as the Ouse along both the Escrick and York moraines, and the scattered group around York suggests that this site may have had more significance in the iron age than has been thought hitherto.

The Arras culture burial rites are to be compared with rites found on the continent particularly in eastern France and must represent a considerable influx of new people as well as new ideas but again there is evidence to suggest merging with native traditions. Stead has noted that whereas the Arras culture burial is usually contracted and was so at the earliest known site (Cowlam) the burials from other La Tène areas of W. Europe are universally extended.[36] The practice of contracted inhumation was persistent in east Yorkshire; examples occur in Anglian cemeteries and even in one of eighth-century date. Another of seventh-century date includes burials which are not only contracted but also contain joints of pork. Contracted burials with joints of meat had been known in the early bronze age, and although the evidence is in favour of cremation rather than inhumation in the late bronze age and earliest iron age, the possibility exists that a continuance of the tradition of inhumation in this period also lurks in the many undated contracted burials found by earlier excavators without distinctive grave goods.

In addition to the burials square ritual enclosures have been identified at Garton Slack rather larger than the barrows. Here also large numbers of chalk figurines have been found of a kind which have been recorded elsewhere in east Yorkshire and can now be recognised as belonging to the Arras culture: stylised human figures, often with sword and shield.[37] Separate ritual burials of complete animals, particularly young ones, sheep, pigs, ox and in one case even deer, are another feature which must have implications for the agricultural economy of these people. The evidence for arable farming is substantial; but cattle, pigs and sheep probably formed the basis of social wealth.

Direct evidence for the iron age economy from the form and extent of fields is difficult to assess. Patterns and landscapes

are known from the numerous air photographs, but it is very
difficult to date the different features revealed, and even when
they include square barrows aligned on or even attached to
field boundaries, alterations and additions to a complex which
started in the iron age may completely distort its evidential
value.

Grain and granaries from Staple Howe, granaries from
Grimthorpe, silos from Scarborough and fields altering the
direction and form of the later iron age dikes do indicate
arable farming in the earliest iron age. The eight or more
magnificent silos excavated by Brewster at Garton Slack and
other late iron age examples prove that arable farming had its
part to play in the economy of the Arras culture. Fields are
associated with settlements such as that at Butterwick.[38] At
other sites drove-ways, leading from the central area of a
settlement to funnel out into pasture, protect arable fields
from encroachment by cattle, as at Blealands Nook (fig. 6).
This particular site is probably Romano-British but the native
economy that survived into the later period must have its
origins in what was there before. Fields and settlements at
Hayton are overlaid by the first-century fort. There is enough
evidence to show that arable farming was important but not
enough to show to what extent. Challis and Harding have
plotted the distribution of bee-hive querns in northern
England and although these continued into the Romano-
British period and like the air-photograph patterns are
difficult to date, the lighter distribution over eastern Yorkshire
compared with the Pennines or the North Yorkshire Moors
must reflect a native agriculture less concerned with corn
growing.

Major dike systems stretching across the Wolds and
limestone hills were associated by Piggott[39], who regarded
them as ranch boundaries, with the pastoral economy implied
by the evidence from the north Yorkshire site of Stanwick.
Closer study of the east Yorkshire dikes shows them to be an
amalgam of works of different periods and purposes. But a
sufficiently large residue remains, which belong to the Arras
culture and which are land divisions, to show that a
completely enclosed landscape had developed with separated
areas for settlement, cemetery, arable and pasture. The

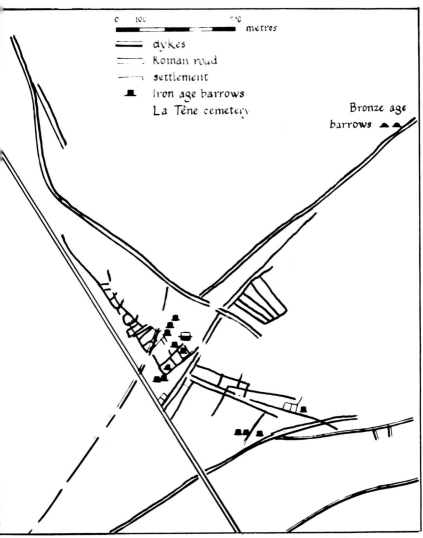

6. Plan of settlements and fields at Blealands Nook, between Fimber and Wetwang, a Romano-British farm but of an iron age type

7. Air photograph of an iron age settlement at Butterwick

boundary dikes are of a size to restrain animals but badly sited for human defence. Many can be dated by association with square barrows, and they provide almost as clear a characteristic to distinguish the Arras culture as the barrows themselves. It should be noted that the distribution is practically identical with that of the barrows except that the dikes extend across the Howardian Hills. Dikes are also found north of the limestone hills on the North Yorkshire Moors but forming systems that are much simpler and without many of the distinguishing features of the Wold dikes.

The Parisi

The equation of the 'chariot' burials of east Yorkshire with the Parisi of Ptolemy was first made by John Phillips in 1852 and although doubted more recently has been carefully argued and accepted by Stead.[40] There can be no doubt but that the area ascribed by Ptolemy to the Parisi included most of the area known to have been occupied by a uniform and distinctive late iron age culture in the immediate pre-Roman iron age. Even if the shifts in emphasis noted by Challis and Harding could be taken to imply a new invasion bringing with it a new tribal name, the underlying unity of the tribe would still be that of the Arras culture. The distribution of that culture as shown by the square barrows (fig. 4) is identical with the former East Riding, with the addition of the limestone hills bordering the north side of the Vale of Pickering. In the absence of sufficient air-photograph cover it is possible that the Howardian Hills, with their similar underlying geology and numerous dykes, should also be included.

Ptolemy, after describing the Brigantes, whose territory stretches from sea to sea, and amongst other places includes York, continues 'near whom and around Safe-haven Bay are the Parisi and the town of Petuaria'.[41] The town of Petuaria has long been identified with Brough on Humber and an inscription confirms this.[42] Safe-haven Bay is cross-referenced in the list of coastal landmarks previously given by Ptolemy, where between the Humber mouth and the river Wear three places are listed, the headland of Ocellum, the Bay of the Gabrantvices (also called Safe-haven Bay), and Hill-fort Bay. Ptolemy uses the same Greek words (here translated Safe-haven Bay) in both entries, but the cross reference has often been missed in the past by those using the Latin translation, which uses different Latin words in each entry. Richmond[43] regarded the Gabrantvices as a sept of the Brigantes but in view of the cross-reference they must be regarded as belonging to the Parisi.

In attempting any identification of the coastal points the changes in the coast south of Flamborough since Roman times must be taken into account. A strip about a mile wide has been lost since about A.D. 600. Spurn Point is subject to a cycle of about 250 years during which it grows larger, is breached by the sea, and then starts to grow again in a position slightly further west. West of Spurn Point on the north bank of the Humber there has been considerable land reclamation.[44]

Ptolemy gives latitude and longitude for both Petuaria and the coastal places. These cannot be relied on to give more than approximate relative positions, but as Horsley noted in 1732:[45] 'Whoever compares his *Ocellum promontorium*, *Abi ostia*, and *Petuaria* one with another, will find that Spurnhead, and the lower part of the estuary of the Humber, and Brough are not very disagreeable as to their relative position and distance.' The main objection to the identification of Ocellum with Spurn was also posed by Horsley. '*Ocellum promontorium* is *Spurnhead* rather than *Flamborough-head* in *Yorkshire*; though it is odd that either of these should be omitted by *Ptolemy*. Perhaps the neighbourhood of *Burlington Bay*, Ptolemy's *Gabrantvicorum sinus*, may have occasioned the omission of Flamborough Head.'

Safe-haven Bay is a very apt description for the present Bridlington Bay. T. Hinderwell in 1811[46] said 'Bridlington Bay is well known to the coasters, as the safest and most commodious of anchoring-places on this coast', a coast notoriously short of natural harbours. Any period of stormy weather will still see ships riding it out in Bridlington Bay. The question is whether the sea had already broken through the morainic ridge linking Barmston and Flamborough to form the bay. A harbour is mentioned at Bridlington soon after 1100, and the Danes Dyke, probably constructed in the fifth or sixth centuries A.D., implies by its siting that the sea had already broken through. If it had formed by then, the bay in Roman times would have been a relatively deeper indentation into the coast line than it is today, with a more distinct southern cheek, part of which survived as an island to be marked on Lord Burleigh's chart in the sixteenth century.[47] The headland would seem to be much more a component part of such a bay than the dominant feature of today. Reference to the distribution map of square barrows (fig. 4), with its heavy concentration behind Bridlington adds support to the argument that when Ptolemy places the Parisi around Safe-haven Bay he is intending Bridlington Bay. Hill-fort Bay is usually taken to refer to the estuary of the Tees, dominated by the hill-fort on Eston Nab, which at its mouth has more the appearance of a land-locked bay than an estuary, but Stead's suggestion that it was Scarborough, and named after a fort on Castle Hill, is a possible although not so attractive alternative.[48]

Ptolemy directly identifies only two places within the territory of the Parisi but it so happens that these two places lie diagonally at the south and east extremities of the area of the Arras culture as defined by the square barrows. Within this area there are two further place names referred to in other sources. *Derventio* is mentioned in the Antonine Itinerary and the *notitia dignitatum*, and *Delgovicia* in the Antonine Itinerary and in a corrupt form in the Ravenna Cosmography. *Derventio* is to be identified with Malton, the only military site on the river Derwent known to have been occupied in the fourth century. The Derwent clearly gives its name to the site and the *notitia* tells us that it was a fourth century military site. *Derventio* is also linked with Brough (*Petuaria*) by the name of the unit stationed there by the *notitia*, which is the *numerus supervenientium Petuariensium*. *Delgovicia* is less easily identified but should lie somewhere south of Malton and north of Brough.

Perhaps there is another clue to the nature of the Parisi in the derivation of three of these names. The *Gabrantvices* are interpreted by Jackson[49] as meaning the riders or cavalry-men, a name obviously suitable for the pre-Roman culture already described, but one more suitable as an epithet for the whole tribe than a distinctive name for part of it. Jackson refers to an alternative explanation where *gabrant* is interpreted as a diminutive rather than a participle, and the name would then be ironic in intention: the 'colts' or 'kid fighters'.

Delgovicia could, like the *Gabrantvices,* refer to a subdivision of the Parisi, the *Delgovices,* with a similar type of ironic name, fighters with thorns for spears.[50] *Petuaria* is derived from a root meaning four and probably implies that the Roman town took its name from one of four subdivisions of the tribe, as with the *Petrucorii* in Roman Gaul, whose four subdivisions derive from the pre-Roman Celtic tribe.[51] The calling of this subdivision by the unimaginative name of the fourth suggests that it is an addition at a late stage in their development to a people already divided into three groups. Brough lies at the edge of an area where the distribution map of square barrows shows that already before the Roman conquest resettlement had begun of lands waterlogged earlier but becoming available again for use. Reference to the distribution map also indicates three areas with heavy concentrations of square barrows which might represent the three other divisions; west of Bridlington, north-east of Malton, and the Arras to Beverley area. The district around Brough does not show a similar weight of concentration. The important collection of pre-Claudian imported material at North Ferriby emphasises the importance of the Humber ferry, which will have grown with the establishment of the Roman province to the south, with a consequent enhancement of the status of the people who controlled it. The two distribution maps of the late La Tène period showing Belgic (fig. 8) and native material, published by Challis and Harding,[52] emphasise the Brough area in a way the square barrow map does not. That map, after all, shows the distribution of one type of monument over some five centuries, and a district which only came to the fore at the end of that period would naturally not be so strongly marked as others. The implications of the name do appear to be borne out by the archaeological evidence.

In summary, an area occupied in the pre-Roman period by a distinctive La Tène culture contains on its south and eastern limits two places described by Ptolemy as belonging to the Parisi, whilst a third place to the north is associated with the presumed *civitas* capital by the name of the unusual military unit that was stationed there at the end of the fourth century. It is reasonable to assume that this area, which is equivalent to the former East Riding with the addition of the limestone hills opening on to the north side of the Vale of Pickering, is that of the tribe. Ptolemy assigns York to the Brigantes and it is logical therefore to assume that the west boundary in his time was the river Derwent, and to exclude the York and Escrick moraines in spite of their square barrows. A doubtful area is that of the Howardian Hills, but since this is clearly part of the hinterland of Roman Malton it is probably best to include it.

Another factor which it is impossible easily to evaluate is the extent to which military controlled areas intrude into the territory of the *civitas*. Indeed the very status of *civitas* can be disputed, and the only certain, indisputable, Roman administrative unit is the *vicus Petuariensis* in the extreme south of the area.

2. History: A.D. 43-367

Little is known of the effect on the Parisi of the establishment of the Roman province to the south. The events that led up to the Roman conquest of the north are usually described, as they are by Tacitus, from the point of view of the main actors, the Brigantes, the tribe whose vast and diversified territory lay west and north of the Parisi. Something must be said about the Brigantes and their relationship to the Parisi in order to understand what happened to the smaller tribe wedged between the Roman frontier and their larger neighbours. The Brigantian economy is usually summarised as pastoral, poor and lacking in agriculture,[1] but there were areas such as the magnesian limestone belt along the western side of the Vale of York and adjacent land, which was suitable for arable farming and capable of supporting a fair population, as the recent air surveys by Riley[2] suggest it probably did. It is this area, possessing a large hill-fort at Barwick-in-Elmet,[3] which was eventually to contain the *civitas* capital at Aldborough. Square barrows of the Arras culture come almost to the site of York, assigned by Ptolemy to the Brigantes, but do not cross the Ouse, and it seems clear that the people to the west were sufficiently strong to set a limit to further expansion of that culture. Hartley[4] has argued that Cartimandua, the pro-Roman queen of the Brigantes, had her seat somewhere in the vicinity of the Vale of York rather than at Almondbury near Huddersfield. He points out that the revolt in south-west Brigantia in A.D. 48[5] meant that her control there must have been weak, and that the coins formerly ascribed to the Brigantes, the main evidence in the past for Cartimandua at Almondbury, have now been shown to be Coritanian.[6] Barwick-in-Elmet is the most probable place for Cartimandua's seat.

The site which Wheeler[7] has convincingly identified as the
place where her main rival Venutius made the culminating
rally of his tribesmen and allies in A.D. 71 is Stanwick, lying
somewhat to the north of the area proposed for Cartimandua's
base. The earliest part of the site is the Tofts hillfort of 6.6. ha.
dated by Wheeler to within twenty years of the Roman
invasion of A.D. 43. Its construction is probably to be linked
with the first breach between Venutius and Cartimandua in
the early fifties. It is interesting that amongst local wares the
excavators found imports from southern Britain. The thin
percolation of Belgic objects northwards to Stanwick is, as can
be seen on the map (fig. 8), entirely eastern. Except for York
and Aldborough, where the objects may well be survivals into
the Roman occupation, the finds are in Parisian territory or in
the northern area of Brigantia which was controlled by
Venutius. His trade connections with south Britain are

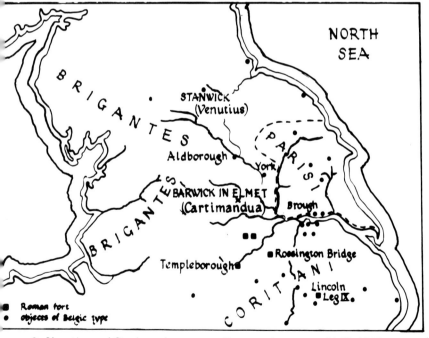

8. Venutius and Cartimandua: map to illustrate the events of A.D. 69-71.

through the agency of the Parisi and illustrate why Cerialis' main attack came through their territory rather than that of the Brigantes.

Wheeler places the first enlargement of the fortifications at Stanwick in the period *c.* A.D. 50 to 70. They now enclosed some 50.3 ha. of level pasturage with adequate water supply, for the defence of a large body of tribesmen and their herds. The final phase, unfinished when it was probably overrun by Cerialis' attack, was much larger and enclosed 282.3 ha. These phases are to be linked with the different stages of the quarrel between Venutius and Cartimandua and the Romans. Cartimandua's troubles began when she surrendered Caractacus in A.D. 51. This led to war with Venutius which lasted to the end of the governorship of Didius Gallus in A.D. 58. The Romans intervened at first with auxiliary troops and then with a legion under Caesius Nasica.[8] In A.D. 69, when the Roman world was dissolving into civil war and the British legions were weakened and divided, Venutius seized his chance. Assisted by revolt among Cartimandua's own subject, and calling in aid from outside he put Cartimandua in a dangerous position and forced her to summon Roman protection. 'Some of our auxiliary troops, cavalry and infantry, after meeting with indifferent success in a number of engagements, finally succeeded in snatching the queen from danger. The throne was left to Venutius, the war to us.' So Tacitus,[9] but Statius, in a poem in honour of the son of Bolanus, the governor under whom this intervention took place, refers to forts established and trophies won in battle from the British king. Statius' words, poetic and exaggerated though they are, have been used to suggest a greater share in the Brigantian war than Tacitus accorded to Bolanus.[10]

How did the Parisi stand in all this? They are usually regarded as philo-Roman but on slight evidence. Richmond[11] pointed to their receptiveness of Roman goods, and the facts of their position between Brigantes and the Romans which rendered their adherence to Rome beyond doubt. The first quality they also shared with Venutius, whose hostility to Rome did not lead him to spurn Roman luxury goods. In 69 their position was radically altered, with the Romans across the Humber weak, the Brigantes hostile to the Romans and

Venutius' castle-building at Stanwick bringing him much prestige. Frere[12] has more cautiously lent support to the 'other scanty evidence' by citing the fewness of the forts built in their territory but the recent discovery of the fort at Hayton and the possibility of others weakens the argument.

The Parisi are unlikely to have intervened before 69, nor is there any need for Roman interference to have involved them. The fort at Templeborough has produced Neronian pottery[13] and Rossington Bridge,[14] if pre-Flavian, may have served as a base for the legionaries under Caesius Nasica or, as Hartley[15] has suggested, both may fall into place as the watch on the Brigantian borders after the intervention of Gallus in support of Cartimandua. The newly discovered forts on the river Went,[16] as yet undated, could reflect the activities of either Gallus or Bolanus. For clearly even on Tacitus' showing Bolanus' intervention was more than Wheeler's 'cutting-out raid'.[17] There is no evidence for any onslaught on Venutius' stronghold at Stanwick before A.D. 71. Cartimandua was defending her own base south-west of York and therefore Roman intervention must have been limited to that area and that approach.

In 69 the Parisi were no longer in a position that rendered any action on their part difficult if not disastrous. Venutius is said by Tacitus to have called in aid from outside, possibly, as Frere suggests, from the tribes of southern Scotland, but not because 'all other directions' were 'ineligible'.[18] Venutius had at least trade connections with the Parisi, and help from that quarter, as a glance at the map (fig. 8) will show, could be much more effective against Cartimandua than any number of tribesmen trekking down from Scotland. The enlargement of Stanwick does certainly demonstrate that Venutius now had a much larger army to accommodate than before, but Parisian auxiliaries might also have to retreat onto his prepared base.

The Tacitean language of the Agricola in describing Cerialis' campaign, *aut victoria amplexus est aut bello*, 'embraced within the range of victory or war',[19] briefly and very aptly describes the direction of Cerialis' campaign round the outside of the Brigantian heartland that had been more directly approached before. The quickest route to Stanwick led in its initial stages through Parisian territory and forts

along the line of approach at Brough, Hayton, and possibly
Stamford Bridge attest the route, and Malton the need to
garrison and control the Parisi.

Brough was the subject of excavations before the war, and
more recently by Wacher.[20] Wacher records both a temporary
camp of unknown size with associated stores depot, and its
replacement, a permanent auxiliary fort (fig. 9) of 1.8 ha.,

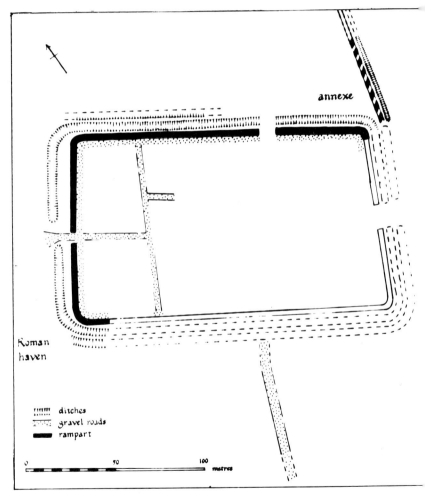

9. Brough on Humber: the Flavian fort

both of early Flavian date. It is archaeologically impossible to distinguish between Bolanus and Cerialis, and Frere's[21] suggestion of the possibility of ascribing to Bolanus the early fort at Brough and at Malton is incapable of proof. But it seems more probable, for reasons already given, that the operations of Bolanus were on the west side of the Vale of York and that the camp and fort represent the campaign of Cerialis and the consolidation that followed. The choice of Brough in preference to the Ferriby crossing, besides the advantages of the local topography, must also have depended to some extent on the arrangements already existing on the south side of the Humber. Stead has suggested the possibility of a Claudian fort at Old Winteringham[22] and there was certainly early occupation there. The possibility that the road-head and this settlement had already caused a move away from the Ferriby site for the Humber crossing before the Romans occupied Brough is emphasised by the discovery of native settlement at Brough preceding the Roman fort.

At Hayton, some 24 km. along the line of the Brough to York Roman road, but a little south-west of the road itself at the crossing of Hayton Beck, there is another auxiliary fort of similar size and date to that at Brough, but this time no temporary camp. The fort was revealed by air photography and has been excavated.[23] It lies on the sands at the foot of the Wolds, a little north-west of the Goodmanham to Etton gap through the Wolds followed by the now disused line of the York to Hull railway. This gap clearly had importance for the Parisi, and the concentration of square barrows in this area (fig. 4) indicates the heavy native population that required the garrison. The fort itself intruded onto a native site (fig. 11); the excavators found part of its ditch system and a ritual animal burial.

Cerialis' direct route north to Stanwick would follow the east side of the Vale of York along the line that was later consolidated as that of the road forking from the Brough to York road near Barmby Moor to cross the Derwent at Stamford Bridge. Here a 'kiln', discovered but not understood in 1954,[24] can now be interpreted as a military oven set in the back of a clay rampart with cobble base. An air photograph taken by the Ordnance Survey shows the crop-mark of the

10. Air photograph of the fort at Hayton

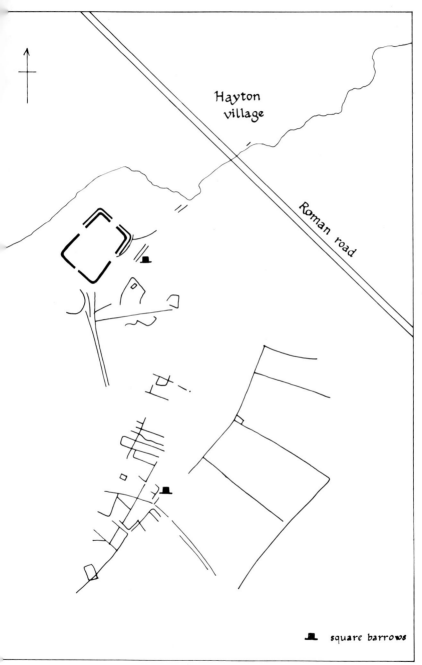

Hayton
village

Roman road

square barrows

11. Hayton fort and iron age settlement

east corner, the shadow of part of the south-east rampart, and enables us, with the position of the north-west side fixed by the river terrace and part of the ditch still visible at its foot, to trace the size and dimensions of the fort (fig. 12). Its area of 1.8 ha. is much the same as that of the forts at Hayton and Brough. There is no dating evidence at present, but the probability is that this fort, like the others, is Flavian, and like

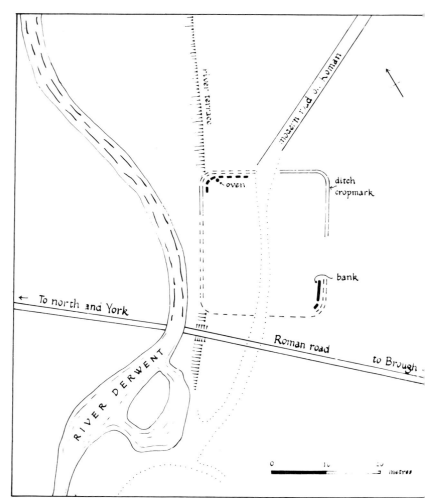

12. Fort at Stamford Bridge

Brough was consolidating the position of an earlier temporary fort. The position is carefully chosen. The fort commands the river at a point where there is a natural flaggy ford across it,[25] and although the rampart where the oven was found has had to be built up against the natural slope the siting of the fort makes good use of the river terrace.

These forts guarded the Roman line of communications to the north from attack from the higher ground of the Wolds. The fort at Malton is more concerned with the control of the Parisi themselves. It was excavated under the direction of Dr Corder in 1927-9, and further excavation has taken place since the war, mainly in the *vicus*. The earliest occupation recorded by Corder was 'an extensive pre-fort occupation outside the fort ditches over a very large area, certainly not less than 22 acres in extent and probably much more'. This produced pre-Agricolan pottery, coins of Vespasian, and stamped tiles of the Ninth Legion.[26] Corder suspected legionary occupation and Frere[27] has suggested a thirty-acre fortress of the Longthorpe type. Closer analysis of Corder's report however suggests that the occupation was not uniform over all the 22 acres (8.9 ha.). There were timber buildings outside the north-east gate belonging to this period, with some suggestion that there might be more extending under the old railway line. South-east of the later fort, stretching from the defences north-east of the south-east gate to the bottom of Orchard Field, a distance of some 76 metres, was an occupation layer of early Flavian date and more timber buildings. Occupation from the north-west and south-west of the fort, however, was more limited and could be better described as a casual scatter. Wenham,[28] excavating immediately to the south-east of and outside Orchard field, discovered what he regarded as the ditch and rampart at the south corner of the Flavian fort. What he found would have included the early occupation recorded by Corder south-east of the fort but nothing south-west of the gate. Moreover the rampart and ditch were too slight to belong to anything the size of a fortress of the Longthorpe type. 'The defences of this camp bore a remarkable resemblance to those of the earliest Flavian camp at Brough – a V-shaped ditch some $4\frac{1}{2}$ ft. wide and $2\frac{1}{2}$ ft. deep with a 10 ft. wide rampart behind it.'[29] These defences must be either those of a temporary camp, or the annexe of a fort which overlapped the eastern quarter of the later fort. Such a fort and annexe together need not cover more than 3 to 4 ha. to include the more intense of the earlier occupation recorded by Corder. The casual scatter, if it needs explanation, could be referred to civilian occupation which must from the very beginning have begun to grow up outside the fort. Malton was in an area of heavy iron age settlement, as Wenham's discovery of chalk figurines of the Arras culture type illustrates. The ditch which Corder found a little to the north-west of that found by Wenham and which remained open into the second century was probably the defence of the Agricolan annexe. Thus at Malton, although we have clear evidence of occupation from the earliest Flavian period, there are doubts both about the size of the fort and about the kind of unit which occupied it.

Cerialis clearly considered that the Parisi needed a garrison of some size. Were there other forts as well? Three of the forts are spaced along the road north and logically one should expect the series to continue and to extrapolate a fourth fort within our area at the crossing of the river Foss somewhere near Stillington, possibly concealed under the site of the priory at Marton. The distribution of square barrows (fig. 4) implies a considerable native population at the head of the Hull valley. Rodwell, in a recent study of the Antonine Itinerary,[30] has considered Iter I as a military tour and suggested that Delgovicia was a fort and in this area. Fieldwork has also demonstrated an aqueduct leading from springs at Burdale which could well have served such a fort. If so it was a site of some permanence and outlasted the Flavian period. But the slightness of the evidence should be stressed, and there is a non-military site that the aqueduct could have served. The ability of a cavalry regiment at Malton, the centre of a fine road system, to control the good riding country of the Wolds would render such a fort less necessary, unless indeed it were an alternative site at one of the periods when Malton was not garrisoned (fig. 13).

Agricola and after

The early Flavian forts, with one exception guarding the lines

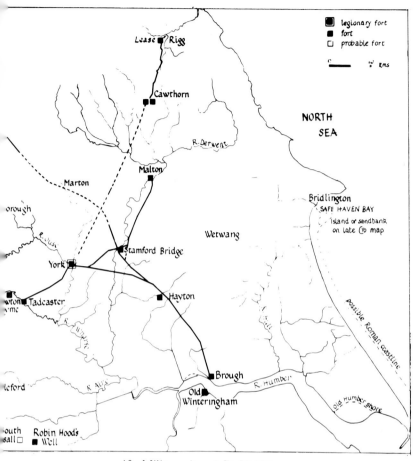

13. Military sites, A.D. 50-150.

of communication, and a consolidation under Cerialis of his campaign camps, were not destined to last long. The campaigns and conquests of Agricola required the troops further north. The fort at Brough was abandoned although the stores depot there probably continued. Hayton was abandoned and so too, if it was Flavian, we can assume was any fort at Stamford Bridge. Malton however was not abandoned and, whatever it had been before, was reorganised as a cavalry fort of some 3.24 ha. Hartley[31] has suggested the possibility that the north Yorkshire moors were garrisoned also at this time at Lease Rigg. Excavation[32] has recently

revealed an elongated fort with annexe to the west. All the
pottery from the site falls within the period A.D. 70 to 120. If
so, it is interesting that the road to Lease Rigg, although it
crosses the northern end of Parisian territory, does not
originate from Malton but from York. Malton was concerned
with the Parisi and not with the peoples on the Moors.

The removal of all the garrisons except one from the
territory of the Parisi by Agricola could provide a reason for
the fortified farmsteads, such as those at Langton,[33]
Rudston,[34] and Seamer,[35] which seem to date from this time.
There is also evidence from the north-eastern edge of the
Wolds of land-division *per strigas*, an old-fashioned form of
land-division which was still used in some of the provinces at
this date.[36] The grain requirements of the fortress at York had
led to possibly enforced changes in the agriculture of the
Wolds from one with a mainly pastoral emphasis to one with a
more arable one, and to some confiscation of land.

Under Trajan the legionary fortress was rebuilt at York in
A.D. 107-8 by the Ninth legion, who were replaced in A.D. 122
by the Sixth. Hartley[37] has placed the withdrawal of the Ninth
from York nearer the first date than the second, and the bulk
of the Sixth at work on Hadrian's wall is not likely to have
seen York before 128. York, in other words, was effectively
without a garrison during the troubles at the end of Trajan's
reign and the recovery afterwards under Hadrian. That
disturbances affected our area is indicated by the need, felt at
least temporarily in A.D. 125, to re-occupy the fort at Brough
to defend the line of communications.[38] Further indications of
trouble come from Malton. Here the fort garrisoned by the *ala
picentiana*[39] was also rebuilt in stone, presumably at the same
time as York, but suffered destruction and burning not later
than the second decade of the second century. The garrison
appears to have been withdrawn thereafter, although the *ala* is
attested in Britain in a diploma of A.D. 124. That the seat of
disturbance locally may have been among the less developed
peoples of the North Yorkshire Moors, rather than among the
Parisi, is hinted at by the possibility of a reoccupation of Lease
Rigg in the early second century. The occupation at
Cawthorn Camps, on a commanding bluff overlooking the
Moors to the north, where, on two separate occasions within

ten years, legionary detachments set up labour camps to
construct forts which were left unfinished, was probably
Trajanic. Richmond,[40] who excavated the camps, regarded
them as part of training on manoeuvres rather than as
evidence of military planning. It may however be the case that
there was an intention to install a permanent garrison here
but that the threat of this sufficiently pacified the people
against whom it was directed and the decision was rescinded.
Alternatively manoeuvres and building activity were intended
to be a sufficient threat, and proved to be, at any rate for the
time being.

The dates are vague, and the pottery from the sites requires
a modern assessment and correlation before we can fit the
evidence from Cawthorn, Lease Rigg, Malton and Brough
into a coherent pattern. All the sites except Lease Rigg were in
the territory of the Parisi, and although the main disturbance
may have lain further north, the need to reoccupy the fort at
Brough, even for a short period, suggests that, even if not
involved, the Parisi were not altogether trusted.

The lack of further garrisoning of the Moors and the
removal of the garrisons at Malton and Brough imply that
whatever remedial action was taken was fairly successful. At
Brough the first developments of the civilian town now begin
and in the later Hadrianic or early Antonine period fairly
widespread building activity took place when the theatre was
built. From the theatre we have a surviving inscription which
indicates that the community had now a definite official
Roman status as the *vicus Petuariensis*,[41] whether or not it was
also the *civitas* capital of the Parisi. It was now also fortified by
a rampart and ditch which enclosed an area extending further
to the north than that of the later town defences. Fortification
at this date of an urban site is unusual and this has led
Wacher to suggest that the site of the *vicus Petuariensis* must be
looked for elsewhere, and that the fortified site at Brough was
a stores depot or a naval base. There is no direct evidence for a
naval base at Brough and it seems altogether too drastic a
solution to regard the theatre inscription as a stray from some
other site possibly as far distant as North Ferriby.[42] Brough
prima facie ought to be the original site of the *vicus Petuariensis*
and its theatre. The underlying assumption beneath Wacher's

suggestion of a naval base is the undeniable importance of Brough as a port site and sensitive communications centre at the crossing of an important estuary. Was the Roman answer to the twin problems of the need for defence and a lack of available manpower to provide a garrison, to organise an unusual urban community including military veterans amongst its citizens?

The further question as to whether the organisation of the *vicus Petuariensis* also implied the establishment of the *civitas* is a controversial one.[43] References to Petuaria in the Antonine Itinerary and in the Ravenna list do not contain the tribal suffix which is usually, though not always, attached to the name of a *civitas* capital; nor, it is argued, is *vicus* the appropriate status for a *civitas* capital. On the other hand the theatre inscription can be restored, on the basis of a C on the left side panel and the presumption of a P on the missing right side panel, to include a reference to the *civitas Parisi*.[44] As Birley noted in his original assessment of the stone, the magistrate who erected it was an *aedilis* whereas a normal *vicus* would only possess joint *magistri*.[45] On the whole the balance of the argument seems to lie with those who favour a *civitas Parisorum*, but clearly there is something unusual about both *civitas* and *vicus*. The withdrawal of garrisons from both Brough and Malton left no garrison for a period after the first quarter of the second century in the territory of the Parisi and this would be consistent with the organisation of the Parisi as a *civitas* at this time. A villa had developed at Welton already at this period, and although the other villas of which we know the history, in the north of our area, do not really begin to develop and prosper until the third century, there are already signs of growth on some of the farms which were to develop in this way.

The period without a garrison at Malton was only destined to last for some forty-odd years. The Antonine wall in Scotland was evacuated about A.D. 155 and a serious crisis in northern England led to the despatch of reinforcements for all the three British legions from the two Germanies. Hadrian's Wall was again put to use and the Sixth legion was working there in A.D. 158. It seems that Malton was regarrisoned at about this time, as Hartley confirms on the basis of both the published and unpublished pottery from Corder's excavation.[46] It is not clear whether this was the result of a simple reversal of the abandonment of this and other sites, or whether there had been widespread repercussions to the south of events further north. Equally it is far from certain whether the Parisi were to any great extent affected by the weakened hold on Britain that resulted from the withdrawal of troops from Britain by Clodius Albinus at the end of the second century in his attempt to make himself emperor. The defences of Malton were certainly repaired at the time of their reoccupation and it would be safest to put the reconstruction of the north-east gate at the same period, but a slightly later date at the beginning of the third century is possible, and has been adopted by Wenham,[47] who also puts the reoccupation of the fort at this later date.

The name and character of the new garrison is not known, but it retained the size of the fort and the line of its earlier defences, repairing and where it was necessary, as at the north-east gate, rebuilding. The new defences, like the old, were in stone but the internal buildings were in timber.

At Brough the second phase of the town defences, on a different line to the first, dates from the end of the second century or even into the early third and can be safely associated with the Severan reorganisation which resulted at York not just in the rebuilding of the fortress but also of the civilian town. At Brough there was much internal building in stone but the town walls were of turf-work and timber unlike those erected around other towns at this time. The difference in attitude at Brough, where stone was used for the buildings and timber for the defences, and at Malton where the reverse was the case may reflect the different priorities of soldier and civilian. The civilian settlement at Malton, however, was also protected at this period by a stone wall backed by an earth rampart.

The third and fourth centuries

The third and fourth centuries were a period of prosperity among the Parisi, who became much more Romanised. This is the period of the development of the villas with a mixed economy in which grain played an important part, as the numerous corn-driers found with the villas and with smaller settlements imply. Romanisation was now so complete that Smith[48] could consider Petuaria as a centre of a school of mosaicists serving not only the area around Brough north of the Humber but extending their operations south of the river as well. There is a certain primitivism about these mosaics, which is to a much greater degree a characteristic of the Venus mosaic from Rudston, so much so in that case that the word grotesque might not be out of place.

This prosperity may not have been without interruption, particularly at the end of the third century. From about A.D. 270 there were increasing raids on the south-eastern coastal areas of Britain by parties of Germans from the sea coasts of northern Europe. No doubt the richer areas to the south suffered most and, although the citizens of Brough received an impetus to erect new defences in stone, the work proceeded slowly at first. The guard-room to the north gate may never have been completed to its original design, and work was probably interrupted for a time.When it was finished, at the end of the third or beginning of the fourth century, it was in a new and more up-to-date style of fortification with projecting bastions and gate towers. Wacher attributes this work to Carausius, comparing the Saxon Shore forts. These were part of a defensive system, finalised a few years before A.D. 300, of forts and signal stations along the coast from the Solent to the Wash designed for cooperation with the fleet. From Flamborough Head to the Wash the coast is subject to severe erosion and has lost a considerable strip of land since Roman times so that the absence of forts to control the Humber estuary may be solely the absence of evidence lost to the sea. The extension of the system northward by a series of signal and look-out towers, running from Flamborough Head as far probably as the mouth of the Tyne, was not constructed until the reorganisation of Britain's defences by Count Theodosius. It may well have been the success of the system further south that encouraged the raiders to look further north. The configuration of the coasts of Britain and Europe might have led raiders first to the more southern areas and their richer booty on both sides of the channel, and it was not until the *barbarica conspiratio* of 367 that coasts to the north became insecure. Todd has suggested that south of the Humber Horncastle and Caistor were forts serving a coastal installation, possibly at Skegness, and another Saxon Shore fort covering the approaches to the Humber was at Grimsby.[49] Wacher thinks of Brough as more important as a naval base than a *civitas* capital.[50] It is, however, possible that defences against sea-raiders were not yet needed so far north and, if they were, that a base at Grimsby would do more good than one as far up the estuary as Brough.

Further inland, at much the same time as the citizens of Brough were beginning to strengthen their defences, there seems to have been a systematic military evacuation at Malton. The contents of the granaries were stacked along the north-east rampart north of the gate and systematically burned, leaving a deposit of carbonised wheat in places nearly 30 cm. thick, extending almost to the gate where it was sealed by a fourth-century road. Corder attributed this event to the later part of the third century, *c.* A.D. 280, and the subsequent rebuilding and re-occupation of Malton to Carausius, stressing the large number of Carausian coins found. If, however, the burnt wheat does represent evacuation, then surely the obvious occasion for it is the withdrawal by Allectus of northern garrisons south to meet Constantius. If, in spite of Corder's arguments, it represents destruction by enemies then the occasion for this must also be after the withdrawal of garrisons by Allectus and before the restoration of the defences by Constantius, and would fall into line with the long list of damage on the wall assembled by Frere.[51] Constantius Chlorus would then have been responsible for returning its garrison to Malton and repairing any damage done to the defences before or as a result of the evacuation. The restored fort contained good stone internal buildings roofed with stone slabs and the north-east gate was rebuilt in an imposing manner, a single arch 11 ft. in span being flanked by guard chambers 6 ft. wide.[52] The comparison is not however with the latest gate at Brough, but with the earlier discarded plan, and the possibility that the defences at Brough should also be given a later date to match that proposed for Malton should be considered. The interior of the fort at Malton continued to be occupied until the final abandonment of Northen Britain.

Considerable later modifications took place to the defences and the buildings, shoddy work that Corder attributed to Count Theodosius. But even in the previous period there had been an obvious decline in military standards, with twenty-nine infant burials suggesting the presence of women within the fort. In the civilian settlement, however, the fourth century was a period of prosperity with luxurious houses built and expansion requiring the reclamation of land from the river. These too met with heavy damage in the disaster of A.D. 367. At Brough an end of the urban community may have come slightly earlier. The Hungate excavations at York in 1951-2 revealed on the banks of the Roman course of the river Foss the remains of a wharf and the massive foundations of what had probably been a crane, which had become buried under a bank of silt. Nearby, Roman layers of the late-third to mid-fourth century were succeeded by an accumulation of alluvial sands of which the last two or three feet must represent a considerable lapse of time during which sporadic flooding continued. This flooding clearly began within the Roman period since strata containing Roman material were seen to be interleaved with water-laid silty sand such as would be deposited by the seasonal overflowing of the river. Recorded in this excavation we have the effects of the beginning of the period of flooding and waterlogging that we have already referred to in the first chapter. If it was such at York as to render wharfage facilities unusable, how much greater must have been the effect at Brough so much further downstream and in so much more vulnerable a geographical position. Wacher's excavations produced evidence of a shrinkage of the occupation there to a small area at the south-west corner and the disuse of the defences after the middle of the fourth century. The *numerus supervenientium Petuariensium* recorded by the *notitia* as being stationed at Malton at the end of the fourth century could well have been formed from those evacuated from Brough, or it could already have been formed at Brough and moved when conditions made Brough an unsuitable site for permanent urban occupation. Wacher[53] argues that this transference must have taken place before A.D. 370 and it may well have been responsible for some of the decline in standards noticed at Malton.

3. Communications and Urban Settlement

The importance of water transport in the Roman period is apt to be forgotten by the student, so often bemused by the romance of the Roman road. Yet, in the landlocked Mediterranean Sea around whose shores the Roman Empire grew, the central position of Rome is meaningless without water transport. Horace's satire[1] describing a journey to Brundisium in the company of Maecenas shows that the poet preferred to travel part of the way by boat along a canal rather than by road, and that his companions preferred a longer part of the journey to be by water and travelled by sea to join up with Horace at a port some way down the west coast of Italy. Passengers often found it more comfortable and safer to travel by water: for goods, particularly heavy goods, water transport could be both cheaper and more efficient. The river Ouse has always been important as a transport artery in York's history and played a considerable part in the choice of that site for the legionary fortress. The river in Roman times was tidal above York, and, apart from difficulties that might arise in times of flood, which did not really affect water transport to a dangerous extent before the second half of the fourth century, it was navigable for sea-going as well as for inland transport.

An inscription from Bordeaux on an altar (fig. 14) was set up by Marcus Aurelius Lunaris, who held office in the cities of both Lincoln and York and in A.D. 237 was shipping direct from York, as the phrase *ab Eboraci evectus* implies.[2] The altar itself, carved out of Yorkshire gritstone, probably travelled down the Ouse with him and direct out to sea without any transhipment. The rivers Ouse and Humber have always been

14. Altar from Bordeaux, dedicated by M. Aurelius Lunaris of Lincoln and York

rivers with shifting shoals and the need for pilots with local knowledge means that even without transhipment, many boats would have put in at Humber ports to pick up and set down their pilots. An altar from York records such a pilot in the service of the legion.[5]

> MAT(RIBVS) AFRIS ITALIS GALLIS
> M(ARCVS) MINU(CIVS) AUDE(NS)
> MIL(ES) LEG(IONIS) VI VIC(TRICIS)
> GVBER(NATOR) LEG(IONIS) VI
> V(OTVM) S(OLVIT) L(AETVS) L(IBENS) M(ERITIS)

'To the mother goddesses of Africa, Italy and Gaul, Marcus Minucius Audens, a soldier of the Sixth Legion, pilot of the Sixth Legion, paid his vow joyfully, willingly and deservedly.' The dedication, although it could refer to the countries from which the legionaries were recruited, is in this context perhaps best taken to refer to the origins of the cargoes handled, and illustrates the wideness of the trade which focussed on the Humber. Legionary supplies imply an import trade into York, of which the bulk, as Richmond long ago suggested,[4] would have been wine, but which would also have included Samian and other continental pottery. As well as sailing from Bordeaux, vessels would have sailed direct from and to the Rhine. A dedication was set up near the mouth of that river by Marcus Secundinus Silvanus, a merchant in pottery trading with Britain, who was grateful for the safety of his cargo.[5] This trade included pottery and fine glass as imports,[6] exports of the products of the Yorkshire jet industry, examples of which have been found in Cologne[7], and possibly linen cloth, for which there is evidence that York was a centre of manufacture.[8]

But in addition to calls at the Humberside ports for pilots and convenience, there is also some evidence for transhipment. The dendritic river system contained not only the two main rivers, Ouse and Trent, navigable for some considerable distance inland for sea-going shipping, but also numerous smaller waterways penetrating far inland which could only be served by smaller vessels, and it included access by the Foss Dyke and Witham to the Car Dyke canal and the network of East Anglian waterways.[9] Much of this traffic

would have been fairly local. The service road from the
Langton Villa led not just to the main road to Malton but
beyond to the banks of the Derwent. Pennine gritstone was
shipped down the Aire, as the distribution of large sarcophagi
in this material illustrates. Magnesian limestone was brought
to York down the Wharfe and up the Ouse. The products of
the Fenland, corn and possibly pottery from the Nene Valley,
were brought to York by the Car and Foss Dykes. The river
Foulness served to distribute the wares produced by the large-
scale exploitation of the local clays by potteries at Throlam,
Hasholme and Newport. A possible explanation of the
absence of Throlam wares at York, the nearest large market
by road, which puzzled Corder, may well be that these kilns
were on the northern edge of a larger manufacturing area
oriented towards the Humber and southwards.[10] On the
Humber estuary, by the mouth of the Foulness at Faxfleet,
was a thriving Romano-British community, partly
agricultural, partly pottery-making and partly a port with its
own small harbour. The site was eventually buried under a
layer of flood deposit about A.D. 350 to 370, drawing attention
again to the flooding at the end of the Roman period which
may well have reduced the river traffic to a mere trickle if it
survived at all.[11] The Hull valley, reaching to the fringes of the
northern Wolds, would have provided another useful
waterway.

The evidence for transhipment was pointed out by Corder
and Richmond[12] who drew attention to the numbers of pigs of
Derbyshire lead found in and near Brough. Five have been
found near Brough itself and another at Faxfleet. These may
be evidence of export – heavy articles brought down the
tributaries of the Trent or Ouse in barges and then transferred
into sea-going ships – but stocks were probably also kept at
the ports for local supply inland and, as Wacher has
suggested, those at Brough could have been part of the stock-
in-trade of a ship repair yard or of a ship chandler. 'Mr
George Naish of the National Maritime Museum, Greenwich,
and Miss Honor Frost, who has studied Mediterranean
wrecks, report that it is usual to find some pigs of lead on
board, which may have been used to replace lead sheathing,
anchor stocks or plummets etc.'[13]

The river systems of Yorkshire which fed the Humber were important to both local and international trade and carried a lot of traffic far inland. The map (fig. 1) shows how far they penetrated and how extensive was the system. The heavy floods after A.D. 350 which closed the ports of Faxfleet and Brough struck at the heart of York itself, burying in silt the wharves on the Foss. In the Theodosian period York must have become much more dependant on local supplies of grain, particularly from the territory of the Parisi. The extensive reuse of stone in the late Roman period at York[14] was another effect of the flooding since new stone could not be brought so easily by land as by water. The sixth- or seventh-century addition to the Roman defences known as the Anglian Tower used the inferior corallian limestone from the Howardian Hills which was nearer to York by land, but not by water, than the better magnesian limestone. The possibility of coastal trade should not be ignored and Safe-haven bay, the *eulimenos colpos* of Ptolemy, directs attention to Bridlington Bay. That there was settlement here of some sort is certain and it is towards Bridlington that the road leads which serves the small group of villas south west of Rudston. The mouth of the Gypsey Race could well have provided a small harbour. Coastal settlements south of Flamborough have disappeared with the coast line, but several small sites are known to the north and although none of these is large and all are agricultural yet some may have looked to the sea as well.

The strategic situation of York in relation to its land communications, which involve the territory of the Parisi, is a commonplace of the archaeological literature and has been best described by Richmond.[15] 'In that basin [of the Ouse] the position occupied by York is of the greatest strategic importance. For there the river Ouse cuts through a glacial moraine which forms a low but substantial natural causeway across the wide and marshy valley. The crossing not only affords easy access to the West Riding of Yorkshire and its dales, but furnishes the necessary south-westward connection with the West March and the Roman legionary garrisons stationed along it. York is thus the key position first for control of the Brigantes, secondly for surveillance of the hinterland of East Yorkshire and Lincolnshire, and thirdly for connection with the western military area. It was picked with that unerring eye for the pre-eminent strategic position which places Roman reconnaissance throughout the Empire in a class of its own.' How these basic advantages of topography and underlying geology were transferred to the road system has been described for the routes between York and Lincoln in an old but still stimulating paper by North from which our map (fig. 15) is taken.[16] The East Yorkshire road system has successively been examined by Maule Cole,[17] Kitson Clark,[18] the Ordnance Survey map of Roman Britain, and Margary.[19] The accompanying map (fig. 16), based as it is on more thorough fieldwork and an examination of the records for all periods not just the Roman, together with the advantage of the unrivalled collection of air photographs made available to the Royal Commission on Historical Monuments, differs in detail from those of previous researchers, but none the less the skeleton of the road system remains as it always has.

The most obvious difference from Margary is the loss of his roads 811 and the great part of 810, which provide two alternative routes from York via Stamford Bridge to Bridlington. That part of the route which leads from York to Stamford Bridge (Margary no. 81a) exists. It has been recently found at Grimston Bar not far from its junction with the York to Brough road (Margary no. 2e),[20] and it has long been known west of Stamford Bridge.[21] East of Stamford Bridge, the road can safely be assumed under the straight length of modern road followed by the parish boundary to the sharp bend at Streethouses. Here it joins or crosses the road from Malton, which Margary calls 81a and projects south-west to join the York road, but which recent work by R.C.H.M. now shows to continue south to join Margary no. 80a, the Durham to Brough road, somewhere between Stamford Bridge and Barmby Moor. East of Streethouses the evidence for the road derives from the work of earlier antiquaries who followed the lines of pre-Roman dykes, later coach roads, and parish boundaries. In many places the development of roads thought to follow the Roman line can be traced, as at Kilham where the straightness of the York road can be shown only to have been achieved at the time of the enclosures. It is possible that a Roman road was the origin of the name Garrowby Street, but

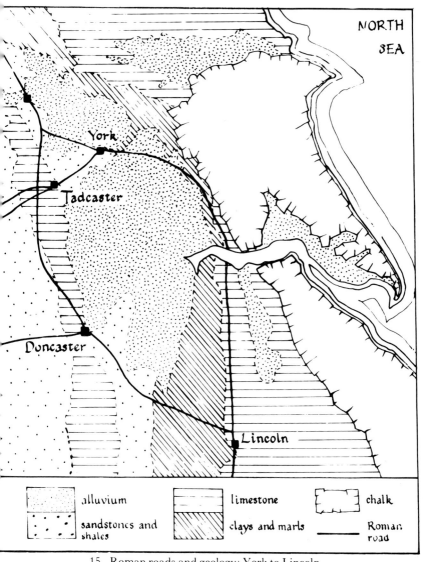

15. Roman roads and geology: York to Lincoln

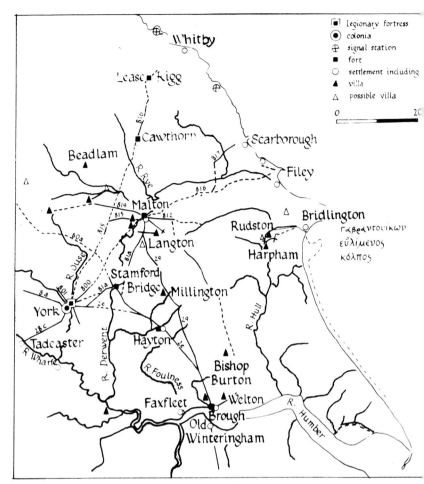

16. Roman roads in East Yorkshire and some related villas

this would only bring the road to a junction with Margary no. 29. Eastwards there is no evidence for, and some against, these lines.

Rather surprisingly Malton and not the *civitas* capital at Brough is the main centre of the road system in East Yorkshire. This may be for military reasons to enable the garrison at Malton to have efficient control over the Parisi. Three of the roads from Malton (Margary nos. 81a, 29 and 813) do, however, lead by different routes to Brough. The importance of Malton as a civil centre is emphasised by the number of villas around it, as many as were around Brough. Wenham[22] has made the interesting suggestion that Malton was the centre for collecting the *annona* or corn tax, and for this the number of roads connecting Malton with a good corn-growing area would be appropriate. Malton is also connected to York by three separate routes (Margary nos. 81a, 800 and 815) whereas there are only two routes from York to Brough (Margary 2e and via Stamford Bridge). Malton was also connected by road with Aldborough (Margary no. 814), Scarborough (817), Filey (816), and possibly Bridlington (812). The road into the North Yorkshire Moors through Cawthorn, however, went direct to York as we have already noted, and the coastal roads may be late, to be associated with the signal stations. The network of minor roads or tracks visible on air photographs in the Knapton area certainly seems to ignore the existence of Margary 816. An earlier road to Scarborough may have led more directly through Old Malton, to which a road leads from the north-east gate of the fort, and have linked with the sharp eastward bend in 817. Dating of a road system is always difficult, but the road 2e and 80a, following as it does the line of Cerialis' advance, ought to be among the first to be established, as well as the road 81a linking Malton with York and Brough. The road east-north-east from Brough emerged probably from the east gate of the town, but also is suitably sited to have come originally from the *porta praetoria* of the Flavian fort. Its eventual destination is unknown although some access must have been available for the number of known sites in Holderness and there must have been a junction with 813.

In addition to the major roads some minor ones are included in fig. 16. Most of these connect villas to the main roads and some may be quite long. The fourth-century road from the Langton villa can be traced for 6.4 km. to the road to Malton, but its line is continued beyond the road by a parish boundary towards the river Derwent which, if it represents a Roman line, would give the villa access to river transport. The road running south-east from Malton towards North Grimston has a less straight course than normal. Branch roads can be seen leading from it on both sides (fig. 17). More

17. Air photograph of Roman roads at North Grimston

complicated is the system of minor roads west of Bridlington. The ridge of the road south-east of Boynton can now be connected by crop-marks and the modern road, East Gate, with the road excavated by Stead north of the Rudston villa. This turned south to pass a possible villa site north-west of Tuft Hill and eventually led towards the Harpham Villa. It also connects with a complicated pattern of roads or tracks (only the boundary ditches are visible) some of which could be of iron age origin. The Wold Gate itself, which used to be accepted as a Roman road, is a rationalisation of the earlier routes and boundaries along the ridge, which is probably post-Roman in date (fig. 18). The shorter road serving the site at Millington, some 400 metres long, survives on the ground both as cutting and embankment. There is in addition a wealth of longer and shorter tracks serving the agricultural sites of the region which have not been included on the map. Some of these are just droveways to lead the cattle through the fields whilst others are of considerable length.

The only documentary evidence which we have for the road system is the final stages of Iter I of the Antonine Itinerary and two names in the Ravenna list which has been convincingly shown to have also been based on a road itinerary.[23] Iter I, as Rodwell has pointed out,[24] is a military route; all the sites identified are military sites except for the *civitas* capitals at Aldborough and, if *Praetorium* is meant to be *Petuaria*, at Brough. The heading of Iter I reads; *A limite, id est a vallo Praetorio usque m.p. CLVI*, and the part relevant to east Yorkshire is as follows:

Eburacum, Leg. VI Victrix.

Derventione	MP VII (6.5 miles or 10.4 km.)
Delgovicia	MP XIII (12 miles or 19 km.)
Praetorio	MP XXV (23 miles or 37 km.)

Praetorio is usually regarded as a corruption for *Petuaria*, but the total distance from York to Brough along the direct road (Margary 2e) is between 45 and 46 km., whereas the distance given by the itinerary is 66 km. This problem has been solved in the past by taking the route from York to Malton (*Derventio*) with the assumption that an X has dropped out before the VII of the distance to *Derventio*, and then from Malton to Brough

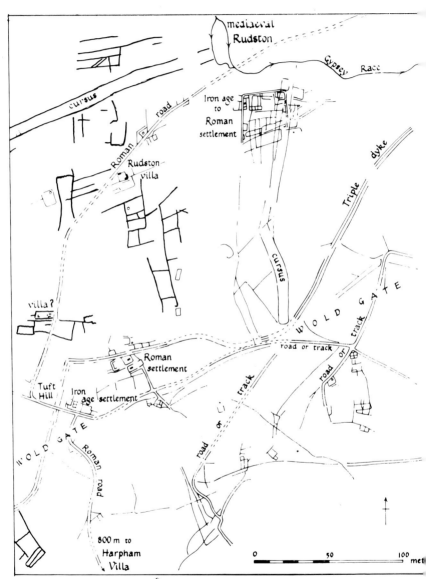

18. Minor roads and tracks south of Rudston

(*Praetorium*) via *Delgovicia*, a site often identified with Millington.[25] The actual distances measured along the Roman roads are: York to Malton 28 km. (18½ Roman miles) along the shortest route; and 31.5 km. (21 Roman miles) via Stamford Bridge. By Margary 815, Malton to Millington is a little over 21 km. (14 Roman miles) and Millington to Brough, 31.5 km. (21 Roman miles). The distances are short *from* Malton and long *to* Malton compared with the Itinerary. The fact that the total mileage in the heading is the total of the individual mileages suggests that there has been no scribal error in the mileages. Millington, which lies off the Roman road, occupies a circumscribed area and is not likely to have been anything larger than a villa. The traditional interpretation of Iter I is not acceptable. The distance by either of the other two routes, Stamford Bridge or Wetwang, is 58 km. (39 Roman miles), very near to the Itinerary mileage of 38 Roman miles. Thirteen Roman miles from Malton would place Delgovicia at Stamford Bridge on the one road and near Wetwang on the other. There is a probable fort site at Stamford Bridge, but the absence of finds of Roman pottery from the area of the probable fort is difficult to reconcile with a long military occupation. None the less an attractive solution would be that the itinerary had originated from a map which showed a road from York to Delgovicia with the mileage VII against it, a road from Derventio to Delgovicia with XIII against it, and a road from Delgovicia to Petuaria with XXV against it. This would be written

Eburacum	
Delgovicia	MP VII
a Derventione	
Delgovicia	MP XIII
Petuaria	MP XXV

The omission of the repeated name Delgovicia at its first use would result in something very like the present form of the itinerary. This would give the correct mileage, placing *Derventio* at Malton, *Delgovicia* at Stamford Bridge, and *Praetorium* for *Petuaria* at Brough. The last is not an easy corruption, but the juxtaposition of *Delgovicia* and *Petuaria* in the Ravenna list, although in the form *Devovicia* and *Decuaria*,[26] does confirm that they are on the same road. Wacher has suggested that *Praetorium* is correct and that accommodation was provided for important officials on tours of duty and waiting for shipment to Gaul and Germany, quoting a possible parallel in *Praetorium Agrippina*. This is not liked by Rodwell[27] or Rivet.[28] The latter suggests that *Praetorium* should refer to York, a natural description for the provincial capital, and that its position in the inventory is due to the confusion caused by the conflation of an itinerary beginning at York with one ending at York. If *Delgovicia* is placed at Stamford Bridge, then the *Delgovices* as a sept of the Parisi would be represented by the burials in square barrows which extend south from Stamford Bridge and along the moraines towards York and Skipwith (fig. 4). There seems to be a much more significant grouping with chariot burials at Middleton and Garton near the Wetwang area where Rodwell would place *Delgovicia*, but perhaps these are a little too near those which must be assigned to the *Gabrantvices* to be easily separated from them.

Thus *Delgovicia* still cannot be placed with finality. It should also be noted that although the identification of Malton with *Derventio* is probable and generally accepted, it is not beyond all doubt. The name is connected by its etymology, explained by Jackson[29] and Smith[30] as the 'River in the Oakwood' or the 'Oak River', with the river Derwent. It is mentioned as an occupied military station in the *Notitia Dignitatum* and as Malton is the only fort on the river Derwent known to have been occupied in the fourth century, the identification seems sound. The name *Derventio* survived into the Saxon period and Bede refers to the assassination at the royal villa there of Lilla whose burial place survives as Lilla Howe on the North Yorkshire Moors. Finds at Old Malton imply occupation there at the right date.

Brough

There are only two places in the territory of the Parisi where urban development can be held with any degree of certainty to have taken place. At Brough was a small walled town, the administrative centre of the *civitas*, with amenities such as a theatre. At Malton a prosperous *vicus* group grew up outside the fort. The theatre at Brough is known from an inscription (fig. 19). This was not found on the building to which it had originally belonged but had been re-used. It was however found in Brough and it is reasonable to assume that its original position was in the same place. The inscription reads as follows:

(on the side panels)   C(ivitas) [P(arisorum)]

(on the main panel)
OB HONOR [EM]
DOMVS DIVI[NAE]
IMP(eratoris) CAES(aris) T(iti) AEL(i) H[ADRI]
ANI ANTONINI A[VG(usti) PII]
P(atris) P(atriae) CO(n)S(ulis) I[II]
ET NVMINIB(us) IANVAR[I]V[S]
AEDILIS VICI PETV[AR(iensis)]
PROSCAEN(ium) [...]
DE SVO [DEDIT]

19. Inscription from the theatre at Petuaria

'The canton of the Parisi. For the honour of the divine house of the emperor Caesar Titus Aelius Hadrianus Antoninus Augustus Pius, father of his country, consul three times, and for the deities of the Augusti, Marcus Ulpius Ianuarius, aedile of the township of Petuaria, gave this ... stage at his own cost'.[31]

The stone is dated to A.D. 140-144 by the emperor's consulship since there is room for three digits and no more. If the expansion of the C on the side panel is accepted, and also the implication that Ianuarius was an aedile and not a *magister*, then we have a date by which the *civitas* was organised, and the *vicus Petuariensis* at Brough became its *civitas* capital. The view of the excavator, strongly expressed in his latest book,[32] was that Brough was not a civilian town but was a naval base, and it is with extreme diffidence that the writer disagrees with someone of Wacher's authority and knowledge both of this site and of Roman urban development in general. The Romans did not install a garrison, naval or military, within the walls at Brough after the final abandonment of the first fort in the second century. Wacher argued that none of the buildings so far excavated find parallels in the houses and shops normally to be found in a town, but equally clearly they do not form the regular barracks to be found on a military site. Most are simple rectangular structures. Three buildings, which have been subjected to more than just trial trenching and which come from widely separated part of the enclosure, produced evidence of prolonged metal-working in both iron and bronze, sometimes on a large scale. There are parallels for the type of building at Wilderspool in Cheshire. It is interesting that there is evidence from Malton at the latest period, when the fort was occupied by a unit with some connection with *Petuaria* and military standards had dropped considerably, that there was metal-working within the fort.[33] Only a small proportion of the internal buildings has been examined at Brough and none within the central area where any public buildings could be expected to be. The large town house such as has been found at Aldborough, or the smaller but luxurious house found in the *vicus* at Malton, have not yet found any parallel at Brough, nor indeed has there been found any house such as Ianuarius, the aedile, might have occupied. The sample examined at Brough is a small part of the whole and the area has been subjected to robbing and agricultural use over a long period.

The streets within the walls do not form the rectangular grid common in towns, and do not have the regularity which is an even stronger characteristic of military sites. Not enough has been recovered to see the street plan as a whole or what the reasons are for some of the irregularities, but some must have been due to the history of the site's development. Whatever the reason for the lack of regularity in the lay-out of the plan at Brough, it is something more likely to have been tolerated in a civilian than a military site. The irregular lay-out of the fortified area, the absence of barrack blocks, and the presence of widely distributed metal-working within the enclosure all argue against military or naval occupation of the enclosure, and the theatre inscription identifies Brough as the town of *Petuaria* and defines its status.

The inscription can tell us something about the inhabitants of the town as well as its status. Ianuarius was probably not a Parisian. His two first names imply that his father or grandfather obtained the citizenship from Trajan, and the possibility is that he was, as Wacher has suggested,[34] a retired soldier. He or his like may have given the town its initial impetus, and a capacity if necessary to provide for its defence. The town was provided with defences at an early stage, soon after the removal of the garrison temporarily occupying the fort in A.D. 125. They enclosed an area that both included the site of the fort and extended north of the later defences. The development of the town was at first slow until the late Hadrianic or early Antonine period when fairly widespread building development took place, including presumably the new theatre. About A.D. 200 new defences were built enclosing a slightly irregular rectangular area (fig. 20) of somewhat more than 5 ha. with asymmetrical gates whose position must to some extent be determined by roads issuing from the gates of the earlier fort. Most of the buildings have a history of reconstruction and use that ended some time in the middle of the fourth century. The defences were converted to stone at

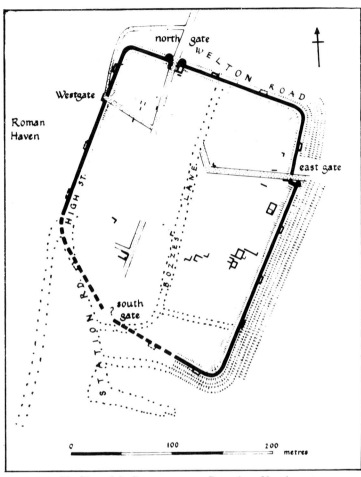

20. Plan of the Roman town at Brough on Humber

the end of the third century, but the work was interrupted and when renewed it was carried out on a grander scale with impressive gate towers and bastions. All was deserted before A.D. 370 except for minor occupation in one corner, the result, as already explained, of the increasing flooding through the second half of the fourth century. It is interesting that

although there is no other evidence of occupation at North
Ferriby since the Claudio-Neronian period, late fourth-
century pottery has been found there. It is possible that the
river crossing moved back to that site in the late Roman
period.

Settlement at Brough was not limited to the fortified area.
The quays lay west of the defences. Corder reported a road
running north-west which Wacher,[35] probably correctly, has
identified with an extension of the quays. Casual finds
indicate the existence of extra-mural settlement north of the
walled town for a width of three-quarters of a kilometre, but
they do not reveal the intensity or nature of such settlement.

At Brough, then, was a small walled town within which
have so far only been found industrial workshops, but which
had public buildings, including a theatre. The layout of the
town is irregular but it was defended from the first and in the
fourth century these defences were on a grand scale. The
harbour area calls for further excavation since this was the
reason for siting the town and provided it with its economic
basis. The settlement extended beyond the walls and around
it were villas, two of which, at Brantingham and Welton, have
been the subject of recent excavations.

Malton

At Malton the development is no more than one would expect
in the *vicus* of a large fort, and the rather grandiose town,
comparable with the *colonia* at York, that has been suggested
by Wenham is clearly out of place.[36] There had been native
settlement on the site before the fort was built and civilian
settlement must have continued adjacent to the fort from its
first occupation but evidence for these early buildings is yet to
find. The earliest occupation found on the site of the *vicus*
during the excavations of 1949-52 was said to be Trajanic.
The published account[37] of these excavations says that the
vicus began to grow and expand in the Hadrianic-Antonine
period when the fort was not garrisoned but Hartley[38] noted
that there was a gap in the pottery corresponding to the lack

of occupation in the fort at that time. Some civilian occupation
must have continued, since *vici* have a tendency to survive and
even grow after the loss of the military site that was originally
the reason for their existence. But clearly the settlement at
Malton languished, even if it did not disappear, when the
economic impetus provided by the garrison was removed.
Unlike Brough, however, the military site was reserved and
reoccupied in the late second century. From then on the *vicus*
grew and prospered.

The main area of civilian settlement lay south-east of the
fort, it probably occupied an area north-west of the river of
about 3.25 ha. (8 acres), and also extended southeast of the
river. Two excavations by Smith[39] and Wenham[40] have added
considerably to our knowledge of its character. The
community was walled, and although only the wall on the
north-east side has been found, a complete circumvallation of
the sides not protected by the fort itself can be assumed. The
wall was substantial, 1.5 metres wide backed by a rampart 4.3
metres wide, with ditches beyond. The settlement as known
was prosperous throughout the third and fourth centuries
when the reorganised fort provided a firm basis for its
economy. But it was not dependent solely on the army. It was
the centre of an area specialising in the production of pottery
and of a rich and Romanised agricultural district, as the large
number of villas surrounding Malton testifies. Wenham has
written a clear descriptive account of the character of the
buildings excavated in that part of the *vicus* north-west of the
river.[41] Like Brough the settlement was not a uniformly
planned one but had grown up rather haphazardly along the
road leading south-east from the fort to the river crossing.
Later another road was added branching from the main road
some 30 metres from the fort gate and taking a more direct
course at right-angles to the fort defences, almost as though
there had been an attempt to rationalise the town plan. There
must have been other streets and alleys, and indeed fragments
were found and recorded but not enough to indicate the plan.
Most of the buildings had a long and complex history. Many
showed considerable sophistication if not luxury. One of the
earlier finds from Malton, or rather from just across the river
in Norton, was this inscription on a small building stone:[42]

21. Building inscription from a goldsmith's shop at Malton

FELICITER SIT
GENIO LOCI
SERVVLE UTERE
FELIX TABERN
AM AUREFI
CINAM

'Good wishes to the Spirit of this Place. Prosper, young slave, in your use of this goldsmith's shop' (fig. 21). Clearly there was a market in Malton for luxury goods. Prosperity is also shown by the nature of some of the buildings excavated, and the town had a piped water supply with wooden conduit pipes lining the road, sloping away from the fort and therefore designed to serve the *vicus*. Water was also drawn from wells. Some buildings had their own private latrines. One building contained a room with figured mosaic floor, frescoed walls, and sculptured Victories on the stone lintel of the door. Two of its rooms, including that with the mosaic, were heated. Other buildings were more utilitarian, with a baker's oven and a kiln possibly for drying corn. Further substantial buildings included one that was probably a bath-house. There was marked deterioration in the buildings in the latest Roman period, and a very late ditch was driven through the former buildings of the *vicus*. This and other crude occupation discovered by both excavators is later than Theodosian buildings and will be discussed in the last chapter. In the late third and fourth centuries the site north-west of the river was fully occupied and there seems to have been some pressure on space, and Wenham suggests that some of the buildings nearest the river were built on reclaimed ground. Certainly the occupation had earlier extended across the river into Norton, along the road south-east for 107 m. or so. The approximate limit to settlement can be determined by the point of junction of roads approaching Malton on this side of the river which ought to lie outside the walled urban area. The sites of these roads within the modern built-up area of the town of Norton are difficult to determine since early finds of metalling are inadequately recorded for position and direction, and some are probably not Roman at all. An approximate position can be fixed by extending inwards the known alignments from outside the town and an approximate limit for the *vicus* based on these alignments is shown in fig. 22. It is surely wrong, as Wenham has done, to force these early finds into a large and extensive grid of streets and infer from this a town of unprecedented size. Beyond the *vicus* there were cemeteries and scattered burials along the approach roads. Amongst and further out beyond the burials were groups of potters' kilns and dwellings, and other suburban development. Outside the main areas of occupation were other scattered civilian sites, and finds come from Old Malton and from modern Malton southwest of the fort. There were also burials north of the fort from which came a tombstone with an inscription:[43]

D(is) M(anibus)
AVR(elius) MA
CRINVS EX
EQ(uite) SING(ulari) AV[G(usti)]

'In memory of Aurelius Macrinus, a former trooper in the Imperial Household Cavalry.' Macrinus only records his most

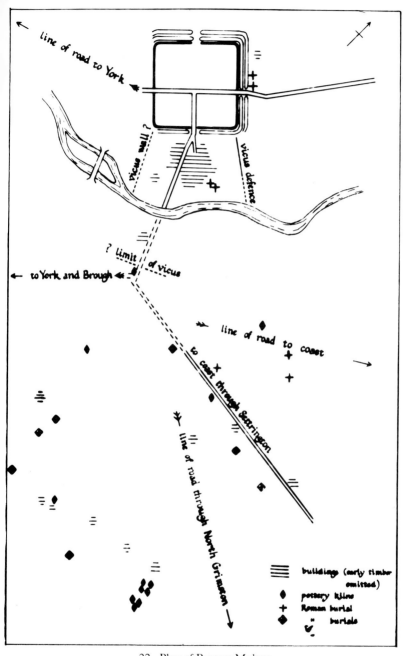

22. Plan of Roman Malton

Legend:
- buildings (early timber omitted)
- pottery kilns
- Roman burial
- " burials

Map labels:
line of road to York
vicus wall ?
vicus defence
? limit of vicus
to York and Brough
line of road to coast
to coast through Scarrington
line of road through North Grimston

important posting, but he probably had served at some time in the Malton garrison and retired there after his service in Rome. Since he does not give a rank, and if his posting at Malton was after his service at Rome he would have come to Malton with promotion, it is unlikely that he ended his days in the garrison at Malton. There must have been a strong veteran element amongst the civilians at Malton. There was also a strong native element. The effigy of a god incised on one altar[44] is Celtic in feel whilst the epithet applied to Mars on another altar is Celtic in language:[45]

DEO MAR(ti)
RIGAE
SCIRUS DIC(avit)
SAC(rum) V(otum) S(olvit) L(ibens) M(erito).

At Malton, then, there was a prosperous urban community, not necessarily larger than the *vici* outside other forts, but the centre of an area devoted to the pottery industry and a rich agricultural area, showing considerable Romanisation.

There may have been other urban communities as yet unrecognised among the Parisi. A road leads east from the group of villas west of Bridlington towards the coast there. The small Romano-British communities at Bessingby were agricultural and the goal of the road may have been a small urban settlement at a port in 'Safe-haven Bay'. They may also have been roadside development such as occurred on Ermine Street at Hibaldstow, south of the Humber. The number and quality of finds of all periods along the road at Hayton may suggest some such development there, possibly originating in the *vicus* of the fort.

4. Rural Settlement

The Romans found in East Yorkshire a fully enclosed landscape divided into large units of mainly pastoral land by the well-known 'Mortimer-' or 'Wold- Dikes'. Within each of the enclosures formed by the dikes were at least two settlements, with a nucleus of folds or yards from which a droveway led through a small area of arable fields into the larger pasture beyond. Much continued with very little change after the Roman conquest. A settlement such as that at Blealands Nook (fig. 6) differed little from many pre-Roman settlements. But the Roman attitude to native agriculture was not entirely *laissez faire*. Apart from the economic effects of the hunger for grain of the large Roman garrisons, which of itself would stimulate an increase in the amount of arable farming, there is some evidence of direct Roman interference.

In the north-eastern Wolds, there is an area of chalk downland bounded on the north and east by the Wold Brow, and on the south by the Great Wold Valley, and on the west by dales cutting into the Wolds from north and south. Here some forty square kilometres are divided by double boundary ditches into a series of concentric semi-circular strips, based on a single ditch following the Wold Brow. These boundaries make careful use of natural features such as the dales cutting far into the Wolds and also of pre-existing iron age dikes. There are also some cross-divisions surviving (fig. 23). The dating of this land division is uncertain within the Roman period, but that it is Roman is clear. There are several rectilinear settlements associated with the land boundaries which, when field-walked, produce surface finds of late Roman pottery. One of these, on Potter Brompton Wold (fig.

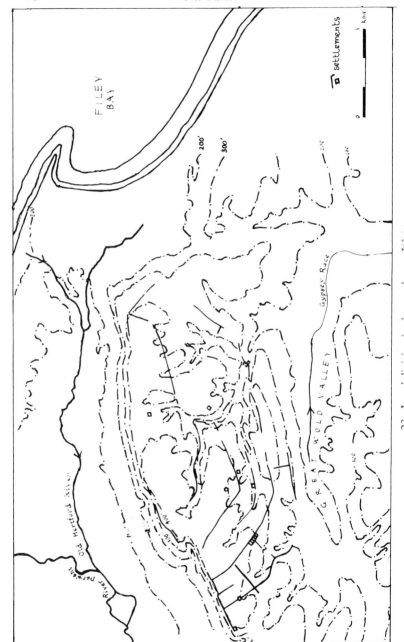

24), is a structural unity with the boundary. Square, 40 by 50 metres, it stands within a severely ploughed bank, still 0.30 m. high but spread to a width of 12 metres. A mound survived within the enclosure until the nineteenth century and the first edition six-inch O.S. map (1854) shows a rectangular feature attached within the south-east side, possibly the trace of a rectangular house. Surface finds included much abraded late Roman pottery including calcite-gritted wares with signal-station type rims and part of a Crambeck bowl. Such surface finds often derive from the last phase of a site's occupation, and it is possible that this farm and the land division of this area belong to a much earlier period. Frontinus describes a form of land division *per strigas*, 'in strips', which was old-fashioned in his day but still used in some provinces; Frontinus was governor of Britain in A.D. 74-78. Another larger and more regular example of this type of land division has been recognised on the other side of York west of Tadcaster.[1] The division probably took place fairly soon after the Roman conquest. Most of the farms belonging to the boundaries are simple affairs within strong ditches. Internal buildings where known are small and rectangular, although at least one has a round hut. A settlement at Cat Babbleton (fig. 24) has grown beyond the original sub-divided rectangle and has developed into a series of enclosures defined by narrower ditches which also include a small rectangular house. At Cansdale there is a much more complicated pattern in which it is difficult to disentangle the Roman from the iron age ditches. Here too are small rectangular buildings of varying size. It is doubtful if the eight known settlements shown on fig. 23 represent all the settlements and it would be dangerous to attempt to make any assessment as to the amount of land farmed from each. It is fairly safe to infer that the farms remained fairly static from their inception to the end of the Roman period. Only Cat Babbleton shows any sign of growth but even that is far from the development to a villa estate that can be seen in other parts of the Parisian territory.

It was from just such another simple rectilinear farm (fig. 25) that the villa at Langton, excavated by Corder in 1929-31, developed.[2] Divided internally into two halves and with a duplicated south ditch, it measured 43.5-45 m. by 26.5-30.5

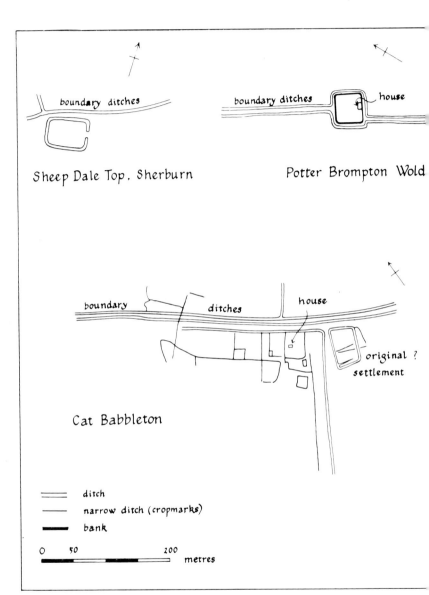

boundary ditches

Sheep Dale Top. Sherburn

boundary ditches   house

Potter Brompton Wold

boundary   ditches   house

original ?
settlement

Cat Babbleton

═══ ditch
──── narrow ditch (cropmarks)
▬▬▬ bank

O   50   200
                        metres

24. Settlements associated with the land division

metres within its ditches, tapering slightly in plan to the east-south-east. The ditch was formidable for a work of this character, 3 m. wide and 2 m. deep, and cut after Roman military fashion, so much so that Corder was prepared to regard it as a small fortlet, an impossible identification, as Richmond pointed out in a review of Corder's publication of the excavation.[3] Equally the work is very different from the kind of native homestead such as are to be found in Northumberland, to which Richmond likened it. The work clearly has a defensive capability. Its Roman rather than native character, in spite of the pottery found within the ditches, is shown by the lead urn with a cremation, recently purchased by the Yorkshire Museum at York, and said to have been found at Langton. Cremation was not a native burial rite among the Parisi. In date all we can say is that at York cremation was going out of fashion by the first quarter of the second century. The possibility is that a retired Roman soldier had been settled on the land here and was using his skills to provide himself with a defence from the possibility of unfriendly natives. Corder dated the farm to the period immediately after the Roman conquest and this would bring it into line with the date suggested for the *per strigas* development in the north-east Wolds. I have already suggested that a suitable occasion for such fortified farms would arise after Agricola's withdrawal of garrisons from the Parisi. Webster,[4] after a re-appraisal of the pottery from the filling of the ditch which was published by Corder,[5] has proposed a rather later date of *c.* A.D. 150 for the establishment of this farm. The pottery, described by Webster as 'an interesting collection of native wares with Romanised types' is not however a cohesive group but derives from a period of occupation with an emphasis on the time immediately before the ditch was filled in and the seat of the farm moved. The pottery from the ditch itself, ignoring Samian and coins which come from elsewhere on the site, would suggest a late Hadrianic date at the earliest for the filling in of the ditch, but that the occupation of the site could be taken back into the first century. Certainly by the time of its replacement, however it had begun, the farm had become fully integrated into the mainly native countryside, using native-made pottery with only a few Romanised types, and also a species of bone peg for which the nearest parallel derives from the late iron-age burial at Grimthorpe.[6]

The farm excavated by Corder was not an isolated example of its type. An almost identical one shows as a crop-mark about three-quarters of a kilometre to the east at Whin Fields (figs. 25 and 26) and there may have been another to the west at Middle Farm where Trajanic pottery was found.[7] Corder found no structures associated with the rectangular enclosure although they may have been obscured by the later fourth century stone buildings. At Whin Fields the air photographs indicate what may be small timber structures.

There were other ditched closes associated with these early farms. At the Langton villa site a row of such enclosures aligned south to north lay to the west with a trackway running alongside to the north. At Whin Fields some of the enclosures in Dale Bottom are of earlier date than most of the others and are perhaps to be associated with the farm there. A contemporary feature probably underlies the parish boundary which still bends to pass round the farm at Whin Fields destroyed in Roman times. Corder also records ditches which

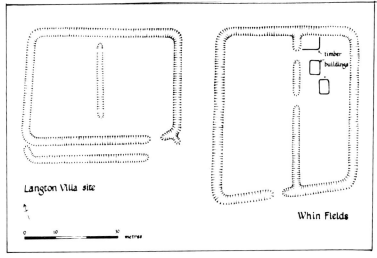

25. Early farms at Langton

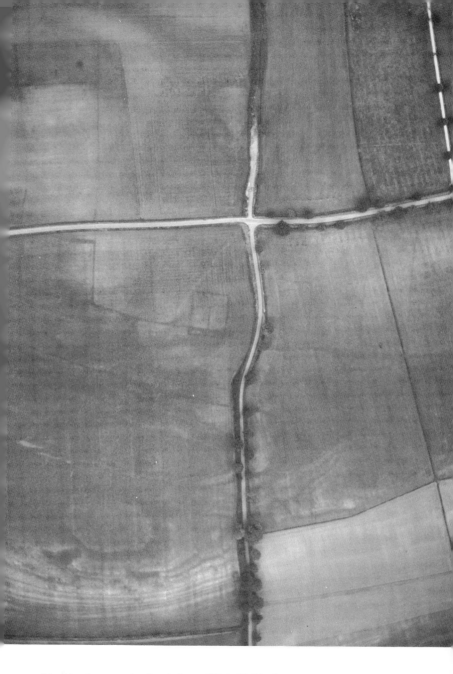

26. Air photograph of early farm, Whin Fields, Langton

do not show up on the air photographs near the Middle Farm site (fig. 29).

Two and a half kilometres to the north of the Langton site, at Brough Hill, Settrington (fig. 27), is another similar but somewhat larger farm alongside a track which can be traced for seven kilometres and joined the road to Malton from North Grimston. It is not certain whether this track was metalled or not, but a large hollow-way or rut implies that any metalling was worn away eventually, probably by the droving of

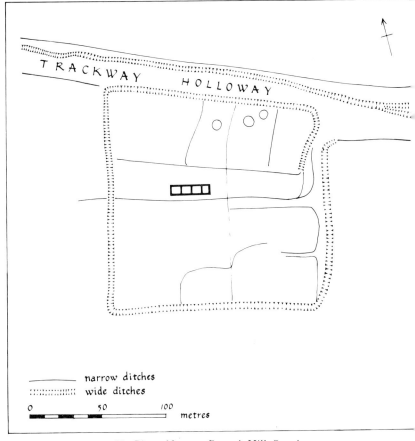

27. Plan of farm at Brough Hill, Settrington

numbers of cattle. Like the other examples this work has two main sub-divisions, although there are further divisions as well. There are three round huts in the north half of 5-10 m. diameter, but the main building was a long rectangular one 28 by 6 m. divided into four rooms (fig. 35).

Excavations at Crossgates, Seamer, revealed a ditched enclosure which the excavators likened to that at Langton, repeating Corder's mistake and identifying it as a Roman fortlet.[8] It produced Flavian pottery and within was the cobbled floor of a house. It was probably a farm similar to that at Langton, but the ditches were stronger. Among the finds was the blade of a sword, suggesting again that the farm was that of a retired soldier. The defensive ditches were abandoned after a short period but the site was not. A timber-framed and stone-roofed building dated from the period A.D. 250 to 370, and was succeeded by stone circular huts of the late fourth century and then by an Anglian settlement of the sixth century. The ditched enclosure measured 61 m. along its east to west axis.

At Rudston[9] an iron age settlement was replaced in the late first or early second century by a rectilinear enclosure, 40 m. across and defined by a ditch about 3 m. deep with an internal palisade.

The evidence, then, from widely separated areas in or north of the northern wolds is that one of the first effects of the Roman conquest on the rural landscape was the development of a series of small farms within rectilinear ditched enclosures provided with military type ditches, associated in one area with land division of a type that was already becoming outdated in the late first century. The possibility is that retired soldiers were deliberately settled on the land to encourage grain cultivation and possibly within a militarily controlled area. In two instances the small farms are known to have developed into villas, at Rudston and Langton, but elsewhere they remained of small size into the fourth century. This settlement could be part of a plan to control the area after the withdrawal under Agricola of all the garrisons in the territory of the Parisi except that at Malton. But if the farms began as planted settlements within a hostile environment, the use of native-made pottery both at Langton and Seamer suggests that relations were soon established on a friendlier basis.

East of Langton and south of Brough Hill, Settrington, is an area within which there are sites producing surface finds of Roman pottery but whose form is more in the native iron age tradition. Elsewhere as we have already seen iron age farms continued into the Roman period with little change. But another type of peasant farm developed among the Parisi more akin to native farmsteads found elsewhere in Roman Britain.[10] An example excavated by Brewster at Garton Slack[11] contained a central circular hut, 10 m. in diameter, within a nearly rectangular ditched enclosure, 49 by 73 m. The ditch was slighter than those of the farms we have been describing. This farm was poverty-stricken, with a complete absence of coins. It dated from the second to third centuries. Similar sites can be recognised from air photographs, such as that near Burton Agnes with two round huts (fig. 28). The closeness of one hut to the lip of the ditch suggests that there was no bank within the ditch although there may have been a palisade.

Such peasant farms were not always as poverty-stricken as that at Garton Slack. Another one, also excavated by Brewster,[12] was sited just below the northern brow of the Wolds at Newham's Pit, Staxton (fig. 28). Among the small finds were samian pottery, *fibulae*, and enamelled objects. There were two ditched enclosures, one within the other. But the larger, outer, curved enclosure seems to have fallen into disuse almost as soon as its ditch was cut, which was in part filled and in part allowed to silt. The ditch of the more angular inner enclosure was kept clean and open. Within this enclosure three round huts were excavated but others may have been destroyed by quarrying before the excavations began. This farm was a completely new intrusion into the landscape about A.D. 75-80. Occupation was not continuous but had two main phases, A.D. 75-90 and A.D. 100-120. There was sixth-century Anglian occupation nearby, and possibly late Roman and fifth-century, but its centre was not located. Brewster thought that the site was not a farm because there were no grain silos, but the occupants could well have been pastoralists. Large numbers of animal bones were found on

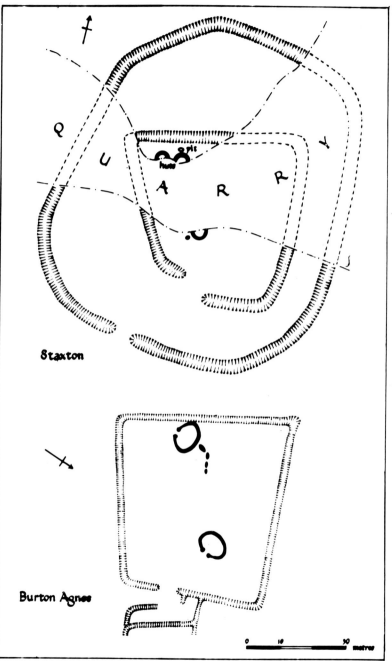

28. Peasant farms at Burton Agnes and Staxton

the site, mainly of sheep but also including pigs and a fair proportion of ox bones. Some grain found on the site was not wheat but cheat and oats probably used as fodder. Brewster noted a correlation betwen the two periods of occupation and the garrisoning of the fort at Malton which also closed for a period from *c*. A.D. 120. He suggested that the site was under military control. If there is any significance in the correlation it must be an economic one. The soldiers provided a market for products from this farm, whether wool for clothing or cattle driven into Malton to provide hides for leather.

Another site of a different character was that excavated by Corder at Elmswell which was occupied through most of the Roman period and possibly beyond. This site will be discussed again in relationship to metal-work carried on there, although it was a mainly agricultural site, with fields, drove roads and corn-drying kiln. It appears to have kept its native character with a Roman veneer, and the famous Elmswell plaque, discovered here, was a piece of late iron age metal-work remounted in Romano-British times, perhaps a family heirloom.[13]

Villa estates

Both at Rudston and Langton the initial farm developed into a villa. At Langton the next stage was the unification of the three early sites into one farm. Three long ditches, very roughly parallel, ran from Dale Bottom for at least three kilometres. The distance between the ditches varied from 50 to 100 m. At Dale Bottom they merge into a group of rectangular fields at right angles to them. In the Bottom itself is a group of smaller enclosures around an open area, a feature which occurs elsewhere among the Parisi. An example at Hayton is seen to be Roman because of its relationship with the Roman road. There is another above the Gypsey Race valley at Rudston. The form suggests a stock-yard (fig. 30).

The more northerly of the three long ditches is the 'South Ditch' of Corder's excavation which cuts across the rectangular enclosure of the first farm and is itself overlaid by fourth century buildings. At Whin Fields the enclosure is

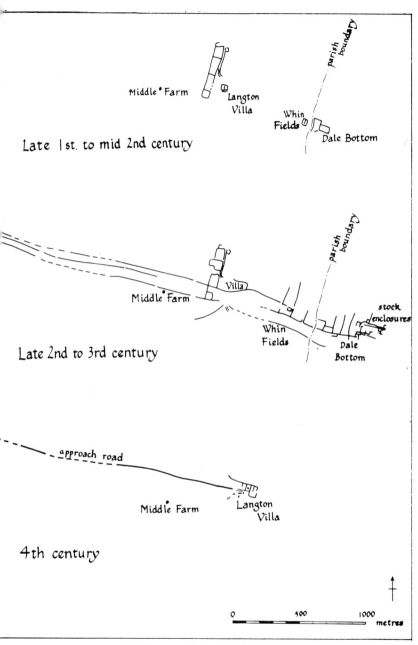

Late 1st. to mid 2nd century

Late 2nd to 3rd century

4th century

29. Crop-mark plans at Langton

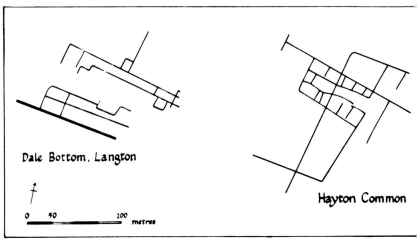

Dale Bottom, Langton

Hayton Common

0   50   100   metres

30. Crop-mark plans of Romano-British stock enclosures

likewise cut by the central of the three ditches. Trajanic
pottery found in one of the ditches near Middle Farm suggests
that early occupation was disturbed there also. These ditches
probably date from c. A.D. 150 when the ditch on the Langton
villa site was filled in. There the 'South Ditch' bows south to
avoid the new farm buildings which must include Corder's
House I, a simple rectangular building 16 by 6 metres, set in
the angle between the east and north sides of a walled
enclosure, extending across and obliterating the earthwork of
the first farm. The west and south sides of the enclosure were
not discovered but since the centre of the bend in the 'South
Ditch' lies to the south-west it probably extended to some
distance west to include buildings, transferring to the line of
timber buildings in the first enclosure to later fourth-century
buildings which, as Webster remarked,[14] seemed carefully set
within that enclosure although their footings were set in the fill
of its ditch. A fragment of walling in line with the bend in the
ditch may be part of the west wall of the enclosure. We do not
therefore know all the buildings on the villa site, let alone what
other buildings there might be on the Middle Farm site. For
although the *tesserae* reported from there may well belong to a
late fourth-century stage, there were probably earlier
buildings on the site.[15] We cannot be sure therefore if Corder's
House I is the only house on the estate or indeed whether it be

a house at all. None the less, simple farmhouses of this kind can be matched elsewhere on the Wolds.

With reservations due to the incompleteness of our knowledge we can suggest an estate, certainly three and probably four kilometres from east to west with a large area of pasture to the north. The main farm was a simple rectangular house with other buildings in a walled enclosure. There was a large stock-yard about a kilometre to the east and possibly other buildings to the west, of the main farm. Some idea of the total size of the estate can be gained from the changing alignments of cropmarks to east and north. These suggest that the estate corresponded very nearly with the later township boundaries of Langton, sometimes as at Dale Bottom extending beyond them, sometimes stopping short. In all it must have included about ten square kilometres.

During the late second or third centuries other buildings were added in the area bounded by Corder's 'North' and 'South.' ditches. These continue the alignment of house I rather than, as earlier buildings east of the house did, adapting their alignment to that of the 'South' ditch. They include a large 'T'-shaped building with a gully that suggests it was used for animals, whether as a stable or a byre (fig. 31).

The fourth century saw the building of a new and more Romanised house on a new site to the north of house I (fig. 32). This was a small corridor house, to which later additions were made and hypocausts added. In its latest stage it possessed mosaic floors unfortunately destroyed by ploughing. The evidence from Middle Farm shows that this was not the only house on the farm and not necessarily the largest. Additional small living accommodation was provided, again with mosaic and hypocaust, at one end of a building whose large door and wagon access suggests its primary use was a barn. A bath-house was erected at one end of the former 'T'-shaped building which had now become redundant. The bath-house was not a very large one perhaps because the house on this site was not that of the owner of this large estate. Another part of the old building was adapted for use as what the excavators, followed by Applebaum,[16] suggested was a threshing-floor but which Webster[17] preferred to identify as a rick-stand. A smaller byre was built to the south of the older

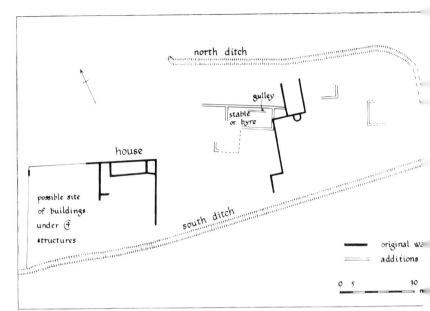

31. Langton villa: second and third centuries

one, with a small internal room for fodder, which was wheat, and possibly also for the cow-man. Applebaum has suggested that the size of the building was such as to provide accommodation for ten to thirteen head on the west side and for eight on the east, the latter probably the ox-teams for ploughing.

Applebaum comments on the careful lay-out of the farm with corn-drying kilns sited to the leeward of the residential buildings to avoid fire risk, and the arrangements for watering and sheltering stock also to the leeward to avoid odours. Certainly the kilns were sited to the east side of the buildings away from the house, and there were external water-troughs in this area showing that part of the enclosure was used for animals, as were also, in all probability, the enclosures to the north, which are visible on air photographs (figs. 29c and 32). Corder commented on the exposed nature of the site, and the villa, like many modern farms on the Wolds, was protected by a wind-break of trees. Twigs were found in the well from oak, ash, alder, willow, elder, walnut, sweet chestnut, sycamore and cherry. Of these species three or four were Roman

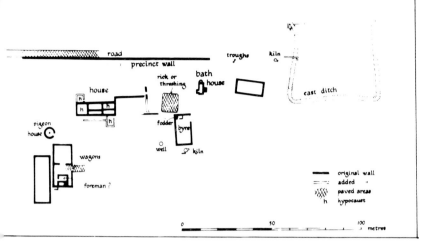

32. Langton villa: fourth century

introductions, another aspect of the impact of the Roman conquest on the East Yorkshire landscape. Sycamore is an unexpected inclusion since Godwin[18] considered it absent from Britain until the sixteenth century.

A small round house was considered by Corder, with reservations, to be a mill, but Webster,[19] in view of the small size and wear of the socket, has made an ingenious alternative suggestion that it is better interpreted as a pigeon-house with a revolving wooden post bearing projecting arms which functions as a ladder to give access to the wall recesses. Such structures are common from later periods in Britain but have not yet been proved for the Roman period. Pigeon bones were not among those recognised at Langton, although the bones from several small unidentified birds were. Livestock also included domestic fowl and ten or more geese. Another fact of interest was the number of deer bones found, from seven or eight individuals. Unlike the other animal bones in the well which represented a sealed deposit of the late fourth century, the deer bones probably came from animals which had fallen into the well by chance, after the site was already deserted. Deer were common in the Langton area immediately after the Roman period and were probably also common during it. Deer were valued both for their meat and their antlers. A mosaic pavement at York,[20] probably from the dining room of a town house, depicts deer in its centre panel and haunches of venison in the corners. At Langton itself there was worked antler tine, cut to form a knife handle. Deer are difficult animals to control and restrain and can cause severe depredation of crops. This may offer an explanation for the size of the north and south ditches of the long fields belonging to the villa; the central ditch was narrower. The north ditch (Corder's 'South Ditch' of the villa) was 2.75 metres wide by 1.8 m. deep below the modern surface. At Whin Fields the north ditch bends south to join the central ditch, and the greater width of that ditch east of the junction is clearly visible on air photographs. With a stockade and bank it could well serve to keep out deer as well as cattle. Deer were not the only predators. Corder records the bones of several small rodents and also of a•cat which was presumably the answer to any problem of that kind. Recent examination of the grain from Malton has shown that it was infected with several different kinds of weevil.

New arrangements were made in the fourth century for the transport of grain from Langton. Not only does one of the barns with its wide doors and paved approach make loading of waggons easier, but the main vehicle access to the farm was reorganised. Previously the access had been from the north but the road through North Grimston to Malton with its numerous feeders had probably become badly worn and rutted by the movement of cattle. Indeed the main road (Margary 813) was probably re-routed at this time north of Wharram-le-Street to lead direct to the Malton to Settrington road (Margary 812), a new fourth-century road, and avoid the steep hill near North Grimston and any rutting of the other road. A new road was built leading west from the villa for three kilometres to the Malton to York and Brough roads, and across them towards the Derwent to have access to water transport (fig. 33). The increasing number of corn-drying kilns during the fourth century indicates the importance of grain growing at this period throughout the territory of the Parisi and it is to this date that those at Langton are to be ascribed. Later in the century there is a possible increase in the labour force and at the same time some of the more northern enclosures ceased to be used. Corder records narrow walls overlying the fourth-century 'East Ditch' and the air photographs indicate several small rectangular buildings just to the north of the area excavated by Corder.

Langton is the villa that has been most completely excavated but it was not the only villa in the Malton area (fig. 33). Others lay just outside the area, at Oulston west of Hovingham, at East Ness, and Beadlam to the north. East Ness is only known from an inscribed stone coffin and small finds, but the inscribed coffin, now lost, should mean the existence nearby of a Romanised site, which in this rural situation could only be a villa. The inscription[21] reads;

TITIA PINTA VIXIT ANN(os) XXXVIII
ET VAL(erio) ADIVTORI VIXIT ANN(os) XX
ET VARIOLO VIXIT ANN(os) XV VAL(erius)
VINDICIANVS CONIVGI ET FILI(i)S
F(aciundum) C(uravit)

'Valerius Vindicianus had this coffin made for his wife, Titia Pinta aged 38, and his sons, Valerius Adjutor, aged 20, and Variolus, aged 15.' This inscription, which probably reflects a

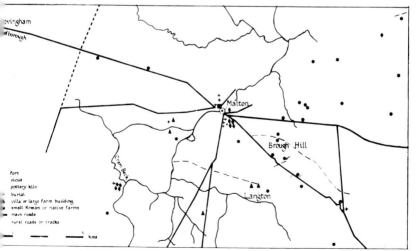

33. Roman Malton and district showing the villas

tragedy such as an illness which wiped out this young family
at one blow, also illustrates the literacy and romanisation of
the dwellers in these small villas. Within our area stone
suitable for making large monolithic sarcophagi is not readily
available from local quarries. Many burials in the limestone
hills are in built-up cists,[22] although another uninscribed
sarcophagus comes from Hildenley just to the west of the villas
at Musley Bank and Rowborough.[23] Another inscribed coffin
comes from the border of the Parisian territory at Hood
Grange[24] 18 km. west of East Ness. This was inscribed by one
Aurelius Serenus to his wife, and came from a small group of
coffins adjacent to a possible villa site. A recent article by
Biró[25] on the Roman inscriptions of Britain commented on the
fact that the practise of setting-up inscriptions in stone was
never accepted by British society at any level. Only a few large
towns, the *coloniae*, and the military centres produce
inscriptions in any quantity. Those from the *civitas* capitals
and the villas are very few. Two distinct social groups are
represented, tombstones set up to common soldiers, and altars
by the mobile military aristocracy, equestrian officers and
legionary centurions who rarely settled in Britain. Only along
Hadrian's Wall under the Severi was there any evidence of
large-scale romanisation of the Celtic population through
recruitment into the army. The contrast in number between
the inscriptions from Brough, the *civitas* capital, and Malton,
the local military centre, would seem to bear out this thesis.
But certainly there was some romanisation of the local Celtic
population at Malton where, as we have already noticed, two
of the altars, both inscribed, reflect Celtic traditions. Here, in
an area where suitable stone is scarce, we have two inscribed
sarcophagi from rural sites, and if Biró is right in his
arguments then this should mean that the inhabitants were of
military origin. Apart from the inscriptions we have other
indications of the literacy of the inhabitants of the villas.
Writing implements (*styli*) have been found both at Langton
and Beadlam (fig. 34).

   The villas at Musley Bank and Rowborough are known
only from casual and poorly recorded finds of the early
nineteenth century.[26] Both buildings appeared to have had
mosaic floors. As at Langton we seem to have had a pair of

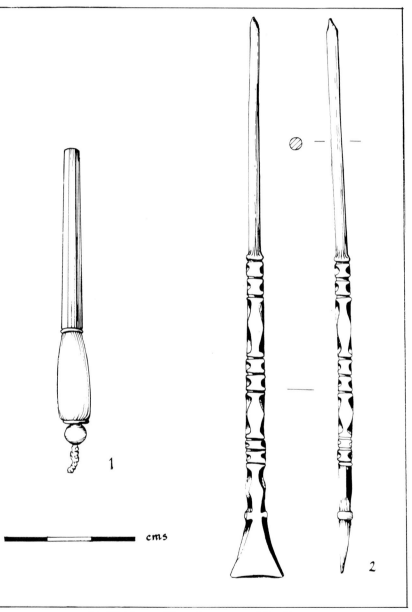

34. Writing styli from Langton and Beadlam

residential buildings on the same estate. The pavements and buildings discovered at Hovingham[27] in 1745 were left in the ground and covered over again, though not before they had been drawn and subsequently engraved. Some of the tesselated pavements at Oulston[28] were removed to the Yorkshire Museum at York, where they still are. Oulston, like Brantingham, had a mosaic pavement along its corridor (10.7 by 3.2 metres) which ran along the front of a series of rooms. At Hovingham both bath-house and house were found, with the mosaic pavement from the latter. Burythorpe is only known from air photographs.

Beadlam is the only villa in this group besides Langton to have been excavated in modern times.[29] This villa is to be preserved as an ancient monument in the guardianship of the Department of the Environment, and the excavations have therefore not gone beyond what was necessary for consolidation and display. We do not know the history of the development of the site in detail. The buildings occupy three sides of a yard. The west range was a corridor house with attached bath-house reminiscent of the houses at Rudston and at Langton of the same date, but larger than both (fig. 35). Most of the floors lacked any mosaics, but one in the north range with a geometric design is to be restored. The east range showed three structural periods. The earliest version, a rectangular building 7.5 by 18 m., was replaced by a single room with apsidal end 7.5 by 11 m. to the centre of the apse. The final construction was in very poor-quality walling built over the destruction layers of the earlier buildings. Some of the rooms in the north range could possibly have been used for non-residential purposes. Some had earth floors and one with an oven was probably the kitchen. None of the buildings could be identified as farm buildings and these are still to be found, not necessarily close to the house. The coin list from Beadlam begins with Hadrian and continues to Theodosius implying a long history for the site. Not all the buildings were necessarily all constructed, or indeed all in use, at the same time.

Among the Parisi corridor houses occur at Langton, Beadlam, Brantingham and Welton, all except the last of fourth-century date. The main house at Rudston seems to be a variant of this type. We do not really know very much about

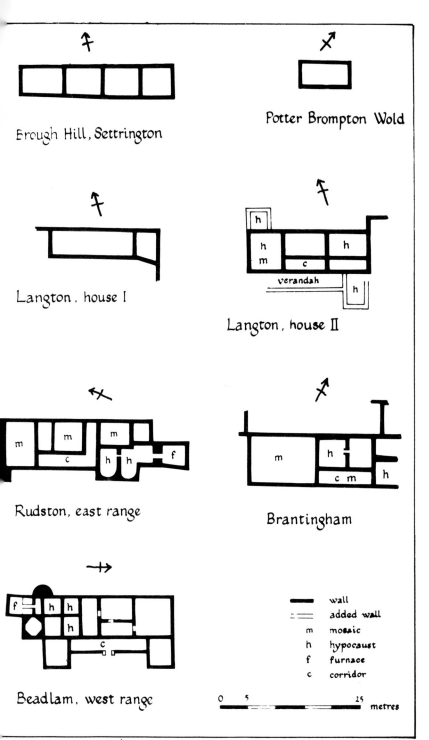

Brough Hill, Settrington

Potter Brompton Wold

Langton, house I

Langton, house II

h

h h
m

c

verandah

h

Rudston, east range

m
m
c
m
h h
f

Brantingham

m
h
c m
h

Beadlam, west range

f h h
h
c

	wall
	added wall
m	mosaic
h	hypocaust
f	furnace
c	corridor

0   5   25
                                    metres

35. House plans from Roman villas in East Yorkshire

the plan of the other villas, but both Oulston and Harpham possessed corridors. The corridor house seems to have been standard in our area for the small Romano-British country house.

Among the small group of villas west of Bridlington, two, at Rudston and at Harpham, have been excavated, and two more, at Grindale[30] and north of Tuft Hill, are barely known, the one from chance finds and the other from air photography. The latter site lies alongside the road which serves both the Rudston and Harpham villas (fig. 18). Native sites and farms used the road and trackways connected with it and are of many different types, the Roman often difficult to disentangle from the iron age, although south of Tuft Hill it has been possible to distinguish the iron age from the Roman nucleus of one group of fields and enclosures on the basis of surface finds. Some of the trackways must have existed before the road, which bends to make use of them. A metalled road was discovered north of the Rudston villa, but in many other places there is a well-marked hollow-way between the ditches, which at times may indicate medieval use of the line, while at others, where the medieval line is different, it must mean the movement of cattle in quantity in Roman times.

Rudston was excavated before the war by Woodward and Steer[31] and more recently by Stead.[32] The history of its development can be summarised briefly. A native iron age farm with round huts was succeeded in the late first or early second century by the defended enclosure already referred to. This had a gateway on the east side with timber doors hung on side pillars, outside which were several road surfaces, evidence that the enclosure had remained in use for a considerable period. Some of the trenches for fences and stockades had not indeed been dug until the Antonine period. Any intervening buildings between the earliest and the fourth-century, developed, villa are as yet unknown in detail.

The fourth-century villa was built around four sides of a yard and had a general south-west to north-east alignment, although for convenience the north-east range will be called east and so forth. The east range, the earliest discovered, had a small bath suite at the south end of a residential block with a large adjacent well. In plan the house could be described as a corridor house with the bath suit replacing the south wing (fig. 35). This range was probably the main house, but a further 'L'-shaped residential block has been excavated on the north side of the yard. Both ranges had interesting mosaic floors. The excavators dated the east range as Constantinian. Dating evidence was not available for the north range but Smith in his study of the mosaics from the site[33] considers that although both belong to the fourth century, the standards of design and execution indicate an earlier date for those from the north range than those from the east. The two sets of mosaics belong to two distinct periods, both in the fourth century, and in Smith's view the one belongs to the first half and the other two the second half of the century. The mosaics are justifiably well-known and have been lifted and are on display at the Hull Museum with those from Brantingham and others from South of the Humber. The largest room of the north range, 4.80 by 4.20 m., had a mosaic floor, 3 m. square of a striking design (fig. 36). The central circular panel displays a victorious charioteer standing facing the viewer in his four-horse chariot. He belongs to the red faction, wears a crash helmet, and holds in his left hand the palm, whilst his right holds aloft the victor's crown or wreath. The four horses are also shown from the front, a difficult position in which to show them successfully. There is a general resemblance with a third century sculptured tomb relief of Neptune in his four-horse chariot from York where it was found re-used in the early fourth-century rebuilding of the north-east gate. The mosaicist has to some extent been more successful than the York sculptor, and his medium has allowed him to show details which are not attempted by the sculptor, such as the head-harness of the horses. The perspective of the pole of the chariot is better. On the other hand the chariot is shown stationary whilst the sculptor has managed to give his horses a sense of movement. Circular panels in the corner of the mosaic display the four seasons, shown as usual as female busts. Two are damaged and two are complete. Smith comments on the quality of the shading obtained by using different coloured *tesserae* on one of the busts although the draughtsmanship is still a little unsure. Oblong panels between the busts each contained a long-tailed bird which it is difficult to identify.

36 Mosaic from Rudston (1) The charioteer

The charioteer is placed in such a position that he was meant
to be seen from the north end of the room. The room was
separated from the next room to the south by a wide and
probably arched opening, the threshold of which was
ornamented by a mosaic panel intended to be viewed from the
south. This panel depicts a *cantharus* or two-handled drinking
vessel between two leopards. The room to the south contained
a mosaic 3.6 m. square of which only the border and parts of
two of the corners have survived. The third room contained a
geometric mosaic with a pattern of intersecting circles.

The mosaics in the east range are notable for the
grotesqueness of the draughtsmanship of the largest, or
Venus, mosaic (fig. 37). This came from the largest room in
the house, 7.16 by 4.72 m., and comprised a central panel,
3.20 m. square, between two oblong panels each 0.73 m. wide,
thus making a total measurement of 4.67 by 3.20 m. The
central panel has as its main feature a nude female figure with
emphasised sexual characteristics. In one hand she holds a
golden apple and the other reaches down to a mirror, both

37: Mosaic from Rudston (2) Venus

attributes of Venus. She is accompanied by a Triton carrying
an upright torch. A torch is a symbol of Cupid and Smith
suggests a degree of confusion due to the legend of her birth
from the sea between Cupid and Triton. Semicircular panels
in the centres of the sides display four different animals, lion,
stag, leopard and bull. Smith suggests that they represent the
four seasons, the Bull spring, the lion summer, the leopard
autumn, and the stag winter. The lion is pierced by a spear
and is accompanied by the inscription:

(Leo) F[R]AMEFER 'The spear-bearing lion'

The bull is also labelled:

TAVRVS OMICIDA 'The man-slaying bull'

In each corner is a bird, possibly a fan-tailed pigeon, pecking a
fruit. In each of the spandrels between the semicircular panels
was a grotesquely drawn figure of which three survive.
    Of the two side panels only one survives complete and this

shows a bust of Mercury central between vines loaded with grape clusters and each arising from a *cantharus*. Of the other panel only the grape clusters are visible, but enough remains from the central feature to show that it was not identical with the Mercury. The draughtsmanship of the mosaics is naive, the grammar of the inscriptions is odd, and there is some confusion between the letters, A, V, and M. The workmanship is semi-skilled and the craftsman barely literate but the subject matter is completely classical.

One of the other two mosaics was geometric in design, with as its central feature a swastika formed of *Peltae* or shield-shaped figures, surrounded by a swastika meander. Only a fragment, albeit a large one, survived from the third mosaic (fig. 38), which floored the dressing-room of the bath suite. This pavement, which probably had an aquatic deity for its centre-piece, displayed fish and kindred creatures. As with the Venus mosaic, the subject matter is completely classical but the drawing is naive.

Smith remarks that the mosaics from Rudston cannot be attributed to any of the fourth-century schools of mosaicists so far identified in Britain. He attaches importance to the discovery in one of the outbuildings in the south range of the villa of what may have been, if not a mosaicist's workshop, at least a place where *tesserae* were produced for sale to mosaicists. There were heaps of *tesserae* sorted by size and colour, with a circular area paved with irregularly shaped flags which may have been a place for 'knapping' the *tesserae*.

The south side of the yard contained other buildings of a utilitarian function besides the one where the *tesserae* were made and stored. One contained no less than eleven corn-drying kilns belonging to the first period of its use and two belonging to the second. The other buildings on the south and west sides of the yard probably belong more to the farm than the house. The lay-out is very different from that at Langton where the buildings are distributed, apparently haphazardly, in a long compound but in fact are carefully sited to segregate noisy and smelly operations to the leeside of the residence. The plan is more like that at Beadlam in that the buildings are grouped round a yard, but at Beadlam the farm buildings have not yet been found and may have been separated from

38. Mosaic from Rudston (3) Aquatic creatures

the residence. At Rudston all are grouped around the same
yard.

The metalled road to the north of the villa was on a
diagonal alignment to it and the accompanying field ditches.
The villa entrance gate, moreover, did not open towards the
road but rather on the east side of the villa, so that there must
have been another branch road serving the villa. The road to
the north can be traced east towards Bridlington and south
towards the Harpham villa. The market for the products of all
three villas along this road may have been some urban
community on the coast at or near Bridlington or grain and
animal products may have been loaded on to the boats there
for export.

Air photographs show that the villa is at the centre of ditch
systems belonging to fields and settlements of different date.
But it is not possible, as at Langton, to sort these out into
different periods related to the structures of the villa. The
early Roman enclosure was based on an already existing ditch
system, and takes the alignment of its south side from that of
the northern of three parallel ditches, the largest of which
contained first-century burials and is probably of iron age
date. They were all three built over in the fourth century. A
group of strip fields, defined by ditches 50 m. apart and of
400 m. known length, are reminiscent of those at Langton and
must surely relate to one phase of the villa's history. Other
field systems may well be iron age, whilst others relate to
small peasant farms whose relationship to the villa is not at all
clear.

The villa at Harpham is less known to us than that at
Rudston and has not been subject to the same kind of
systematic excavation. It was first excavated by Sheppard and
Collier in 1905, and indifferently re-excavated in 1951 and
1955.[34] The villa as known is again of fourth-century date,
since a coin of Constantine (A.D. 305) in mint condition was
found below one of the pavements. The building excavated
appears to have been 'E'-shaped, three wings connected by
corridors, and of some architectural pretension. But the
quality of the excavations left much to be desired and it is not
clear how much of the plan of the building was recovered. As
at Brantingham and Oulston corridors appear to have been

floored with mosaics. The rooms appear to have been somewhat larger than those at Rudston. The pavements had geometric designs, the most interesting in the form of a maze, with a floral centre. The others were of chessboard or fret patterns and some indeed were only the borders of larger mosaics. Fragments of earlier buildings were found, and third-century pottery, as well as other items suggestive of iron age occupation of the site including a bone peg and a chalk figurine.

Near *Petuaria* villas are grouped at fairly regular intervals along the road north from Brantingham to Newbald, with others at Welton and further away at Bishop Burton. At the last place it is probable that there were two separate buildings. Gent[35] who recorded the original find in 1733 refers to the ploughing up of two pavements, the one in the next but one field to the other, i.e. deriving from buildings which were not immediately adjacent to one another.

The villa at Brantingham[36] is larger than any of the other villas so far found among the Parisi and has the finest mosaics. A large fragment of the house has been recovered, an apparently corridor house but with added rooms behind, and parts of an adjacent building also with mosaic floors. The mosaics are related in the general framework of their design, in particular the use of a wheel design, in the standard of execution of the figures, and in the employment of the same or similar patterns, to the mosaics from the villas at Winterton and Horkstow south of the Humber. Smith[37] makes a carefully argued case for the mosaics of all three sites to have been designed in the same workshop which, on the basis of the distribution of the major mosaics, ought to be at Brough, *Petuaria*. Smith indeed refers to the Petuarian school of mosaicists.

At Brantingham the centre-piece in the design of the major mosaic is an octagonal panel displaying the nimbed head and the dalmatic-clad shoulders of a female figure adorned with a mural crown, a *tyche* or the personification of the quasi-divine protectress of a province, tribe, or city. The owner was perhaps a magistrate or official of the *civitas*, or the *vicus Petuariensis*. Considerable painted plaster had fallen from the walls onto the mosaic floor, and this has been reconstructed to show part of the decorative scheme. In their design the wall paintings echo some of the designs in the floors. Liversidge has suggested that there may be a local art school represented in the mural paintings as well as in the mosaics. The villa at Brantingham belonged, as found, to the fourth century and nothing was recovered to illustrate any earlier history of the site. In its mosaics and paintings it reflects the culture of the wealthier members of the *civitas* at that period.

Welton[38] is different. It is much smaller and more integrated into the local countryside. The history of its development is known from a native iron age farm to a late Romanised farm with corn-driers and metalled access road. The simple iron age farm was demolished in about A.D. 100 to make way for a small corridor house, 13.4 by 19.4 m., smaller but not greatly smaller than other houses shown on fig. 35, but very much earlier in date than them. It was demolished in about A.D. 340, but since occupation went on until at least A.D. 400, if not into the fifth century, there must have been another house as yet undiscovered. There were aisled barns and smaller animal shelters in the fields. A total of 13 corn-driers was excavated. In the fourth century, as at Langton, access to the farm seems to have been reorganised and a metalled road built to the south, presumably to link with the road leading east out of Brough. The interesting fact about this villa is the early date at which the corridor house was built compared with Langton, but the 60 m. compound in which it is set is reminiscent of the first farms at Langton and at Rudston. This compound was suppressed in the early third century.

Little can be said about the other villas, north of Brantingham, along the roads running north to York and Malton.[39] Most is known about the southern site at Newbald where Corder dug a trial trench. Stone walls, laid floors, tesserae, painted wall plaster, box-tiles, roof tiles and a gable finial indicate a villa, and the extent of the remains suggests a large one. Occupation lasted from *c.* A.D. 220 to 370 but insufficient was excavated to enable one to be really sure of the dates. The description of the finds at the northern site at Newbald sounds very similar. From South Cave there is only a fragment of tesselated pavement, although a Romano-British smelting site was located further east. The walls reported from Nunburnholme are not necessarily Roman, although Roman pottery was found. An aisled building at North Cave lies west of the roads on the fringe of the pottery manufacturing area.

The villas have so far fallen into three groups, those centred on the fort and *vicus* at Malton, those centred on the *civitas* capital at Brough, and those centred on a possible port or town at Bridlington. The site at Millington is more isolated, although less so if the building at Nunburnholme is accepted as Roman, and if there was a roadside settlement of Hibaldstow type at Hayton. It lies on the north side of the valley of Millington Dale which, unusually for a Wold dale, has a stream and copious springs. A road, at first in a cutting and then embanked, ran down the slope to join the Malton to Brough road (Margary 29) at the point where it crossed the valley floor. A side valley caused the descent and prevented a junction with the main road at a higher level. The place where the buildings were found lies in the angle between the main and the side valley, where there is not a large amount of room. Tesselated pavements, coins and pottery were found in 1745.[40] An unusual feature was a circular building 13.7 m. in diameter with wall foundations 1.5 m. thick. The eighteenth-century discoverers of the site, who were arrested on suspicion of laying out a Jacobite camp, suggested that they had found a temple and were probably correct. Circular buildings are found on villa sites, e.g. at Winterton,[41] but these are slighter buildings, examples of the survival of the earlier round house tradition. We do have examples of such survival among the Parisi, the most remarkable the two very well-built stone round houses of fourth century date from Crossgates, Seamer.[42] But the building at Millington is something different. Not only is it large and the walls wide, but the published plan, if taken literally, would imply that the footings were of monolithic slabs, each the width of the wall. Two column bases were found and the fragment of a pillar. All this suggests something rather grander than the usual villa found among the Parisi. The remains of the other buildings were fragmentary. The plan shows two 'L'-shaped blocks and a square tesselated pavement, all three on slightly differing alignments, which it is difficult to reconcile into one complex. Clearly much was missed that a modern archaeologist would have noticed. The walls were severely robbed. Drake,[43] one of the original discoverers, says 'that it had been the Custom for the Inhabitants of that Village, Time out of Mind, to dig for Stone in the Ground when they wanted'. The possibility is that we have either a villa with a temple of the Brigstock[44] type adjacent to it, or as at Lydney there was a guest house or residential accommodation attached to the temple.

There is no firm evidence of the deity worshipped. Drake[45] notes that 'Very near the Ruins, I have mentioned, are some Springs of excellent Water & so copious, as when joined in one Stream below it, turns a Mill from wh[ich] I suppose the Name of Millington has proceeded. Water being so scarce in this country that the People, in a dry Summer, are obliged to drive their Cattle many Miles to these Springs.' Running water is very much a rarity on the Wolds. The springs at Millington are at present tapped by the local water authority to provide drinking water. In a similar situation on the eastern side of the Wolds the stream of the Gypsey Race attracted pre-Roman religious centres, cursuses, a henge, and the famous Rudston monolith. In the territory of the Brigantes at Well, the excavated bath-house could have been associated with a Roman shrine near the site of what, throughout the mediaeval period, was a holy well. There is scattered, but when gathered, formidable evidence for the survival of Celtic water cults into Roman Britain.[46] There seems quite a possibility that it was some water god or goddess that was worshipped at Millington. The only clue to the date of the building lies in coins of Titus and Gratian found on the site. The associated buildings are more than the mere outbuildings suggested by Lewis[47] but whether a villa in the normal sense of a farm, attracted here by the water, or associated more closely in some way with the life of the temple it is impossible in the absence of evidence to say.

The temple at Millington is not the only evidence for the possible survival of earlier native religions among the Parisi. At Garton Slack,[48] Blealands Nook,[49] Harpham,[50] and Malton[51] have been discovered wedge-shaped chalk figurines of iron age date, images of warriors with swords, usually but not always headless. Stead[52] suggests that the beheading is a magical attempt to immobilise an enemy. At Garton the idols were associated with ritual square enclosures. This wedge-shaped form is repeated in a small sculpted stone (fig. 39)

39. Sculpture of horned deity from Kirby Underdale

from Kirby Underdale of Roman date which has attracted comment by Haverfield, Collingwood and Ross.[53] The stone is small, 31.5 cm. by 21.6 tapering to 11.4 cm. Carved in low relief on one face is a crude figure wearing a winged or horned hat, with a club or torch in his left hand and an oval object, perhaps a pine cone, in his right. He is naked except for a girdle, and either a dagger or emphasised penis is also visible. The stone is a local sandstone.

Water must have been a perennial problem in the chalk area of the Wolds, and indeed remained so until an improved method of lining dew-ponds was invented by Gardiners of Driffield, well-diggers and fish-pond makers, in the 1760s.[54] It is possible that methods of collecting and storing surface water were known to the Romans but otherwise they would have had, like their successors until the eighteenth century, to rely on pools in the more retentive clays and marls of the valley bottoms or dug wells often very deep. Cattle may well have had to be driven miles to be watered. Both at Langton and at Rudston the villa dwellers relied on wells to provide them with all the water they needed. The quantities of water required for the bath-houses would seem to imply that they employed some mechanical means of raising the water. At Rudston the well is close to the bath-house but at Langton it is some distance from it. Wells had often to be quite deep. Near Millington above the valley a well suspected to be Roman[55] had been driven 24 metres through solid rock to save a relatively short distance to the springs. In Garton and Wetwang Slacks even relatively impoverished peasant farms had dug wells to reach water, here much nearer the surface. An aqueduct of Roman date is known from recent fieldwork, air photography, and old accounts of earlier fieldwork[56] to have run from Burdale Springs for a distance of about 7 km. Its ultimate destination is unknown.

5. Industry and the Economy

It will be realised from the foregoing pages that East Yorkshire was essentially a rural area in the Roman period. Brough, Malton and York were the three centres for which it served as a hinterland. Two of the major lines of communication to York passed through the territory of the Parisi, by road from York to Lincoln and by water down Ouse and Humber to the sea. The *civitas* capital was at the crossing of the two. York is a centre whose presence must not be forgotten although, because it lies outside our area, it must necessarily always be off-stage. Yet together with Malton it must have provided a major market for the products of the countryside. Similarly, to the south lay the much richer and more Romanised territory of the Coritani. A comparison between the illustrations of villas in the volume in this series on the Coritani[1] with those in fig. 35 will at once show the difference. It is no accident that the *civitas* capital lies at the southern edge of its territory. The villa at Brantingham had its main parallels south of the Humber, and the Petuarian school of mosaicists served the area south of the Humber to a greater extent than that to the north. Brough was as much a centre for South Humberside as for the Parisi.

If some of the main markets were outside Parisian territory, so were the main sources of most raw materials other than agricultural products. East Yorkshire is not endowed with good mineral resources. The best metal ores, coal and building stone were just outside their territory, although ferruginous limestone is exposed at the foot of the cliff at Cayton Bay, and oolitic limestone was exported to York. Better timber could be found in the Vale of York although finds from Staxton do suggest that oak was available in the

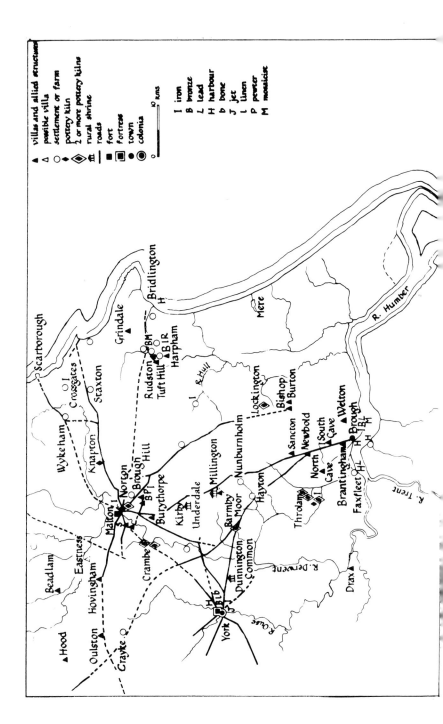

villas and allied structures ▲
possible villa △
settlement or farm ○
pottery kiln ◇
2 or more pottery kilns ◈
rural shrine ⛩
roads
fort ■
fortress ▣
town ●
colonia ◉

0 ____ 10 runs

I iron
B bronze
L lead
H harbour
b bone
J jet
L linen
P pewter
M mosaicist

Scarborough
Hood ▲
Beadlam ▲
Eastness
Oulston ○
Hovingham ○
Crayke ○
Crossgates ○ I
Wykeham
Staxton
Knapton
Grindale ▲
Rudston ○ BM
Tuft Hill ▲ B I R
Harpham
Bridlington H
R. Hull
Malton I
Norton
Brough Hill
Crambe ○
B
Burythorpe
Kirby
Underdale
Millington
Nunburnholm
Lockington I
Bishop Burton ▲
R. Hull
Mere
Barmby Moor
Dunnington Common
Hayton
Sancton ▲
Newbold ▲
North Cave ▲
South Cave
Welton ▲
Throlam
Brantingham ▲ I
Faxfleet H I
Brough ● H B I
York ▣ H B I b
R. Ouse
R. Derwent
Drax ▲
R. Trent
R. Humber

Vale of Pickering. East Yorkshire did possess good pasture, land eminently suitable for growing wheat, clay suitable for potting and excellent communications by land and by water. It is not surprising, therefore, that the main products of the region should have included grain, animal products and pottery, but it is more unexpected that there should be so much evidence of metalworking.

Agriculture

Wheat appears to have been the main cereal grown. The army at York and Malton would require grain in quantity. York could derive much of its supply by water from the south, but supplies from East Yorkshire were nearer to hand. Malton would derive the bulk of its supplies locally. It was a road centre for most if not all the territory of the Parisi and Wenham[2] has made the useful suggestion that Malton was the local centre for the delivery of the *annona*, or yearly corn tax imposed for the supply of the army, which the farmers had to transport themselves. From Malton we do have evidence for the type of grain supplied. The composition of the burnt layer of grain found on the rampart at Malton and dating from the end of the third century had the following proportions in the sample examined:[3]

Various wheats	300
Naked barley	14
Emmer	12
Clubwheat	11
Avena sativa (oats)	5

Applebaum comments 'If the Malton finds were of local derivation, therefore, the adequacy of winter-grazing in the Wolds enabled the ample sowing of winter cereals even at the expense of summer crops', i.e. oats. That oats were also grown is shown by the evidence from the pastoral peasant farm at Staxton, where finds of grain were of cheat and oats, presumably, but not necessarily, used here for fodder. At Langton the corn bin in the byre was filled with wheat.

Langton also provides us with evidence of the proportion of

arable to pasture. Applebaum[4] has estimated that there was room for four ox-teams in the byre, and comments on the ox-bones of five or six individuals from a sealed deposit in the well that they represented the three ox-teams in use at the time. Three teams, on the basis of Columella's figures,[5] were capable of ploughing 300 *jugera* (737,000 square metres) and four teams 400 *jugera* or 983,000 square metres. The third-century strip fields almost certainly also used in the fourth century contained as known 550,000 square metres, but, if additions are made for their probable westward extent and for the rectangular fields at their east end, a figure of some 800,000 square metres is arrived at, i.e. somewhat more than 300 jugera. If we accept the size of the whole estate as being some ten square kilometres, a proportion of arable to pasture of 1 in 12 is arrived at. Comparison with an iron age area for which we can make a similar estimate, at Wetwang, where out of an area encompassed within dikes of some 6 square kilometres, 160,000 square metres were occupied by arable and settlement, a proportion of less than 1 in 33, demonstrates how the Romans had increased the area of arable, by economic pressure and deliberate encouragement. Nevertheless arable still forms a very small proportion of the total, much less than at the greatest extent of mediaeval arable before the growth of sheepfarming led to the reversion of much of it to pasture. At Langton the mediaeval proportion was five of arable to four of pasture and meadow, although of the arable a third would lie fallow each year.

Perhaps the most distinctive feature illustrative of the economic life of the countryside are the corn-drying kilns. The usual form is a 'T'-shaped flue with stoke-hole; above this was a perforated floor on which grain was placed. The roasting or parching of grain was a widespread Roman practice which is referred to by Ovid and Pliny. Among the advantages was the prevention of germination of the grain and a lessening of the risk of rotting whilst the grain was in store. It was also useful for preparing damp or unripened corn for milling. In many northern districts of Britain the practice survived into the nineteenth century.[6] There were other simpler forms of corn-drier in addition to the 'T'-shaped kilns used by the Parisi.

Immense quantities of leather were needed by the army for

footwear, uniform, harness and tents. Evidence from Catterick showed a depot for the preparation of leather outside the fort in the period A.D. 80-120. The large number of animal bones found there would suggest that the raw material was delivered on the hoof.[7] The situation was probably the same at Malton. The feeder roads leading into the road via North Grimston to Malton with their hollow-ways deeply worn by the passage of cattle show the way the oxen were driven to Malton. Much further east the peasant farm at Staxton produced both oxen and other animals, mainly sheep, and as the excavator commented its periods of occupation correlated with those at the fort in Malton. Hides and wool would also find a civilian market. Loom weights are a feature of many sites in the country and at Malton and York. The remains of cloth in gypsum burials at York, however, would seem to be of linen rather than wool, and it is possible York did not provide much of a market for woollen products. Flax is a suitable crop to grow in the Vale of York but would also grow well in the Hull valley. Bone from the animals would have been required in quantity for implements and for ornaments. A workshop for the manufacture of bone pins was evidenced at York.[8]

Pottery manufacture

Throughout the Roman period until the late fourth century the fine wares used by the Parisi were imported from the continent or south Britain. The more utilitarian domestic pottery continued to be made locally. At first the local iron age traditions continued with a few added imitations of Roman types.[9] Probably during the second century specialist centres developed making a better class ware. The local native wares had been of a clumsy dark fabric and were made at two centres associated with Brough in the south and Malton in the north. A third local fabric found at York may also have been made among the Parisi. Hand-made pottery in the native tradition still continued to be made, particularly for cooking-pots, and in the fourth century developed into the wheel-made Huntcliff type cooking-pots which after A.D. 367 became the standard cooking-pot in northern Britain. In the fourth

century a new type of ware began to be manufactured at
Crambeck near Malton and after A.D. 367 took over almost the
whole market for pottery other than cooking pots in northern
Britain. K. Hartley[10] has suggested that this was a deliberate
policy in the province controlled from York of buying pottery
as far as possible from within the limits of that province.

The three main centres for pottery manufacture in the
territory of the Parisi were south of Holme-on-Spalding Moor,
where on the fringe of the Vale of York sands overlie suitable
clays, at Barmby Moor in a similar topographical situation,
and around Malton. The Throlam and other kilns south of
Holme-on-Spalding Moor served the southern area around
Brough. The villa at Brantingham, for example, was entirely
supplied from Throlam, apart from a few colour-coated wares.
Brough also was largely supplied from the Throlam kilns but
it also imported wares from just across the Humber and even
some from Norton. Throlam wares do not seem to have
travelled north to York or Malton, although a road left York
in the direction of Throlam.[11] The kilns were sited near the
river Foulness (fig. 41) and it is probable that the finished
wares were exported in barges southward rather than on
wagons north. The course of the river has to some extent been
lost as a result of the construction of the Market Weighton
canal. The southern end of the canal follows the course of a
former stream called the Frisdyke, one of the many outlets
from Walling Fen into which the river lost itself (on fig. 41 the
streams have been marked as they are shown on Jeffreys' map,
surveyed in 1771-2 before the canalisation). But these streams
themselves result from earlier attempts at draining the fens. It
is difficult if not impossible to recover the Roman course of the
river Foulness through Walling Fen. It is very possible that the
river had been canalised to some extent already in Roman
times and that it followed approximately the line of the
Frisdike at whose mouth a small Romano-British site with a
possible harbour[12] was excavated near Faxfleet in 1962 and
1967. Kiln saggers found here may mean that the community
included pot making among its other activities, but the
saggers could have been left with the pottery as packing
during transport. Certainly Throlam ware was found at
Faxfleet. The earlier course of the Foulness as shown on

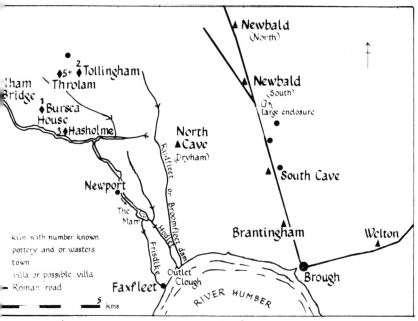

41. Pottery kiln sites near Throlam, and villa sites north of Brough

Jeffreys' map passed within a hundred yards of the kilns at Hasholme, and a tributary led towards Throlam.

The kilns at Throlam were excavated by Corder and Kirk in 1930.[13] Five or more kiln sites are known near Throlam farm, the site of Corder's excavation, two at Tollingham Farm,[14] one at Bursea House[15] and three at Hasholme.[16] Finds of pottery and/or wasters come from a further five sites including Faxfleet. Only a few kiln sites have been excavated out of what must have been a much larger number. The structure of one of the Throlam kilns is shown in fig. 42. The ware (fig. 43) had a very hard grey fabric. The surface is smoothed in a series of horizontal bands between 3 and 13 mm. wide with decoration of lines incised, or burnished on the unsmoothed sections. Products include two-handled storage jars, jars, bowls, beakers and platters, and from Hasholme jars of Dalesware form but in a soft coarse-grained pottery ware or in a hard grey ware without the grit. Corder tentatively dated the operation of the kilns to the second half of the third century

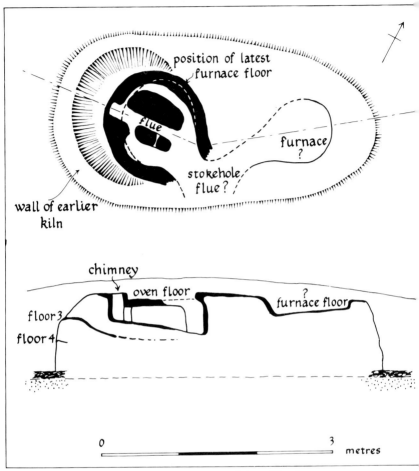

position of latest furnace floor

flue

furnace ?

stokehole, flue ?

wall of earlier kiln

chimney

oven floor

furnace floor ?

floor 3

floor 4

0   3   metres

42. A double pottery kiln at Throlam

but admitted that a greater knowledge of the stratification at Brough would provide better dating evidence. Wacher[17] with that greater knowledge, noted that there is pottery of similar fabric to Throlam from a very much earlier date but that the earliest pieces which could be positively identified as Throlam wares do not occur until the end of the second century. The wares continue into the first half of the fourth century.

The Hasholme, Tollingham, Throlam area is crisscrossed by the crop-marks of agricultural settlement and fields, and some of the ditches of such settlement at Hasholme were dated to the period immediately before or after the Roman conquest. What is not clear is the extent to which agricultural settlement overlapped with the pottery industry. Presumably at some time the farmers discovered the clay under the sand, perhaps at the side of the river bed, and exploitation of it increased with the demand for pottery. The area probably had plenty of timber with which the kilns could be fired. The combination of market, raw material, wood for firing and an easy transport system in the water-ways ensured the economic success of the kilns.

A similar combination of circumstances must have existed in the valley of the Hull but further from any possible market at Brough. That clays here were exploited is shown by the kiln at Lockington.[18] This is away from water transport but not far from the course of the road from Malton through Bainton. It probably served a fairly local market, and produced dishes, cooking pots and jars, similar to those from Throlam and Norton between *c*. A.D. 150 and 240.

The Norton kilns[19] produced similar wares to the Throlam kilns at much the same date in a stone-hard dark grey fabric. The surface is smoothed except for bands reserved for decoration. In addition to types of vessels produced at Throlam, Norton ware (fig. 43) included indented beakers and pots with appliqué decoration. The pot of the latter kind found at the kiln site was part of a face jug but vessels of the same kind from the nearby fort and *vicus* of Malton have smith's tools, a wheel and part of a human figure as their decoration. Besides the grey ware, large hand-made jars and cooking pots similar to those from Knapton were produced. The distribution is uncertain but was probably more than local. Certainly Norton products reached Brough. But the sites which have produced large quantities of the ware and the stratification to date them are local – the fort and *vicus* at Malton, and the villa at Langton. At Malton the products from Norton were predominant from A.D. 220 to 280, and this must be regarded as the *floruit* of the kilns. But those excavated were in use into the fourth century and some of the types are repeated at Crambeck. The Norton kilns went out of use during the first decade of the fourth century. Eight kilns were

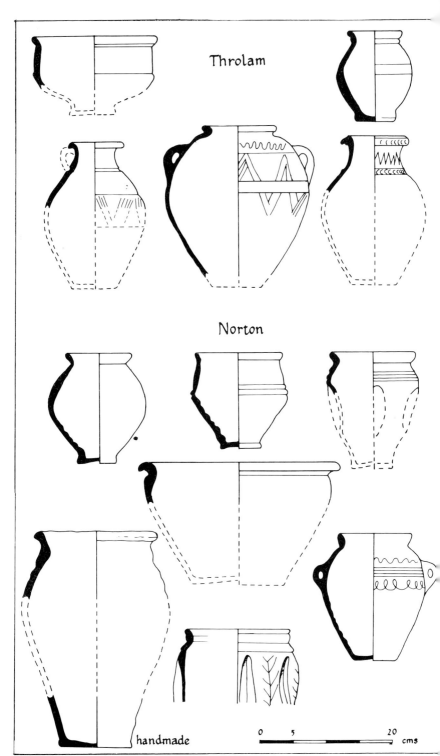

Throlam

Norton

handmade

0   5   20
                                     cms

43. Selected products of kilns at Throlam and Norton

excavated but casual finds suggest that there were several others. A rectangular paved floor built after A.D. 270 and in use in the late third and early fourth century was either the dwelling place or workshop of some of the potters. Food bones included ox, sheep, and pigs together with limpet and oyster shells. Two querns were found on the floor and a 'T'-shaped drying kiln was found nearby. This might imply an agricultural occupation, but such drying kilns could be an adaptation of an agrarian structure for drying pots. A similar drying floor at Crambe,[20] with two pottery kilns nearby but sited on a small fourth-century farm, could have been equally used for parching grain and for drying pots. Coal found at Norton may have been used for firing rather than wood.

Crambeck,[21] some 7½ km. south-west of Malton fort, was a very much larger and more important site. It is usually said to begin in the middle of the fourth century, but the overlap of types between Norton and Crambeck might suggest that it began earlier. The *Geological Survey*[22] notes the existence of a fine potters' earth at Crambeck, and it may well be that a discovery of this better material led to the movement of potters from Norton to Crambeck. The production of fine wares need not have begun until later, but the kilns are not likely to have expanded into the kind of production that they later boasted without some kind of nucleus to start from. After A.D. 367 Crambeck becomes the major supplier in North Britain for all kinds of pottery except cooking-pots. Only a handful of kilns, on the edge of several hundreds visible as crop-marks, has been excavated. As well as possessing the advantage of a good potters' earth, Crambeck is also well sited for transport, as it lies adjacent to the river Derwent and the possible line of a road between York and Malton. The products (fig. 44) included straight-sided grey or black burnished flanged bowls with a wavy band internally below the rim, and mortaria, bowls, jars, face-jugs and flagons in a hard white or biscuit-coloured fabric (parchment ware) painted with orange-red decorations. There was also some imitation samian. Crambeck mortaria have dense ironstone grits. Huntcliff type cooking-pots, although exactly contemporary and used at Crambeck, do not seem to have been made there. Two kilns slightly further south at Crambe[23] look very much as if the

44. Selected products from the kilns at Crambeck

pottery manufacture there was a sideline undertaken on a small farm under the influence of the nearby industrial site. One of the kilns was an adaptation of an earlier domestic oven. These kilns produced ordinary Crambeck types with an emphasis on the straight-sided bowls.

A suggested source for the Huntcliff-type cooking-pots is at East Knapton,[24] ten kilometres north-east of Malton, on the southern fringe of the Vale of Pickering where sands and gravels overlie glacial clays. Yet the Huntcliff-type cooking-pots formed only a very small proportion of the pots found at Knapton. Kilns were not located, but the large quantities of unused pots found suggest that they must have been nearby. The bulk of the material found consisted of hand-made cooking-pots in a thick hard black, buff or brown fabric heavily charged with calcite grits (fig. 45). The type is a descendant of native traditions going back to the late iron age, and from it developed the wheel-made Huntcliff-type cooking-pots, some of which were also found unused on the site. The period when the Knapton cooking-pot flourished at Malton was the third century, but it must have continued in manufacture into the fourth century when it was superseded by the Huntcliff-type. East Knapton alone is not capable of producing the large quantities of Huntcliff-type pots which were made but casual finds do suggest that there was heavy fourth-century occupation in the vicinity and other kiln sites may yet be found.

Finally there is the virtually unknown site at Barmby Moor[25] where at the turn of the seventeenth and eighteenth centuries finds were made implying the presence of kilns. This is confirmed by air photographs, which show that the site was a large one. It lies in an area of sandy ground west of the village of Barmby Moor, between the Roman roads from Brough to York and Stamford Bridge, just north-west of their junction and some 15 km. from York. We know very little about the products of these kilns. The early description refers to the pots as bluish grey in colour having a great quantity of coarse sand wrought with the clay. The obvious market for the ware is York, and it must be looked for among local wares found there. Gillam[26] records the existence among pots found in the Trentholme Drive cemetery of local wares in a grey

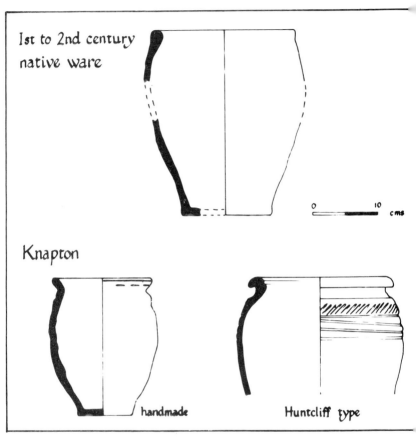

1st to 2nd century native ware

0   10 cms

Knapton

handmade

Huntcliff type

45. First and second century native ware, and wares from Knapton

sandy fabric, butt-shaped jars and jars with flat-topped rims, the latter including some reminiscent of Dalesware in form. Gillam provisionally regarded these pots as the product of a single factory in or near York, which began work in the second half of the second century and continued at least until the second half of the third, producing successively the butt-shaped jars and the two varieties of jars with flat-topped rims. A waster in the same ware but in a differnt form, a small beaker, was found at Gate Helmsley[27] about 8 km. north-west of the sites at Barmby Moor.

Metal-working

Barmby Moor combined metal-working of some kind with pottery manufacture. Finds of slag were made with the original discovery and there have been more recent reports of slag from ploughed fields in the area. Presumably the combination of metal and pottery manufacture is due to the ability of the potters to fire and construct furnaces. York would provide a ready market for either product, and although in the case of the metal-working raw material would have to be brought from a distance, fuel for firing was probably abundant in the vicinity. York had had its own metal workshops[28] in the second century, but there were obvious fire, noise and smoke nuisances in an urban setting for this industry. The York workshop was replaced by a town house in the third century, and although evidence has been found for other industries at York evidence for other metal workshops is lacking.

At Hasholme, too, some smithing was done besides potting. Among the finds from there was an anvil[29] of a type commonly in use in the Roman period, a large tapering block of iron with a flat working surface relying for stability on its weight (13.9 kg.). The Hasholme anvil lacks the pronounced step which on other examples marks where they emerged from the block of wood or stone into which they were set, but no doubt it too was sunk into a similar block when in use. The excavator drew attention to the nodules of iron ore occurring in the sand at Hasholme, as they do elsewhere in the East Yorkshire drift, and wondered if these might not have been the source of the iron worked, but with the excellent transport facilities available it seems more likely that they were imported in the form of blooms from across the Humber.

At Brough[30] there was strong circumstantial evidence for both bronze and iron working within the walled town. This was on some scale and over a considerable period of time. There does not appear to have been any special area set aside for the workshops or at least not a large one, since the evidence came from three separate buildings widely spaced within the walled area. The fuel used appears to have been coal. It is not unexpected that Brough should have along with its other associations with the area to the south of the Humber some connection with the iron working that resulted from the presence of iron ores there. The activity carried on appears to have been smithing rather than smelting although the evidence was not as firm as the excavator would have liked.

At Malton[31] a smith's forge was found in a building built into the north-east rampart of the fort, which after a period of use was replaced by another industrial hearth. There can be no doubt about the fourth-century date of both structures. Outside the fort in the same area a bloomery had been built in the partly filled-in inner great ditch of the fortress. As on this side of the fort the inner ditch had been allowed partially to fill in the fourth century, this bloomery is probably Roman. It is tempting to link the bloomery outside with the forge inside and to link both with the unit whose name associates it with the town of Petuaria and whose station at Malton in the fourth century is recorded in the *Notitia*. The main occupation at Brough ceased about the middle of the fourth century and the unit probably did not appear at Malton until then. Similar activity appeared at a late period in the *vicus*, where two forges were found. Wenham dates this activity late in the Roman period and associates it with a ditch which was ruthlessly dug through earlier stone buildings in the *vicus*. Associated metal working has not yet been proved at the Norton kilns, but such a possibility is hinted at by the decoration on some vessels in grey ware which were probably made at the Norton kilns although the sherds were found in the fort and *vicus* and not at the kiln site. This decoration is appliqué and consists of smith's tools, hammers, tongs, pincers, and perhaps an anvil, as well as wheels and parts of human figures.

Smithing for the purposes of the local community rather than on a commercial scale, was probably carried on in the small Romano-British farms in much the same way as it had been during the preceding iron age. One site which produces evidence for this is at Elmswell,[32] where the agricultural base of the community is shown by corn-driers and by the crop-mark pattern of fields and drove-ways visible on air photographs. The site shows occupation right through the Roman period, with a hint of continuity with the pre-Roman period conveyed by the Elmswell plaque, a piece of late La

Tène metalwork remounted in Roman times, possibly handed down as an heirloom. Here there was evidence for smithing. A sample of ash was analysed and shown to be the sweepings of a smithy floor. An area of laid chalk and gravel had the hearth on its western side. There was also considerable iron slag on the site.

The villa estates like the mediaeval manor probably tried to be self-sufficient in most things, and it is not surprising therefore that they too should produce evidence of metal-working. Recently Goodall[33] has gathered the evidence together from the villas at Langton and Harpham. The evidence from Langton suggests smelting as well as smithing. Bronze objects were made at Langton, Harpham and Rudston. Five crucibles were found at Langton, and four at Harpham with a fragment from a fifth. Rudston has produced the fragment of a mould for a brooch, and Harpham a mould for a ring and several half moulds for producing bronze studs including a composite one (fig. 46). Corder published but did not identify a lathe-turned stone object which Goodall has shown to be the lower half of a mould for making pewter dishes closely paralleled on other sites. It would have been possible by using a number of different upper half moulds, by trimming down a complete casting, by flattening the edge and turning it over to form a thickened rim, to have used the Langton mould to cast virtually all the known rim-types known on Romano-British pewter tableware. Goodall suggests that, in view of the distance of Langton from any source of tin, the pewter was not alloyed at Langton but brought there in the form of pewter cakes such as those that have been recovered from the Thames.

Lead was also found at the Langton villa and it is possible that that was cast there too. The large number of lead pigs found in Brough and its vicinity was used by Richmond and Corder to identify the trading possibilities of Brough and the suggested transhipment for export. There may well have been transhipment, but it is perhaps better to regard the lead as held in stock for local use, perhaps, as Wacher has suggested, at a ship-chandlers,[34] a view supported by the fact that another pig was found at the smaller port at Faxfleet.

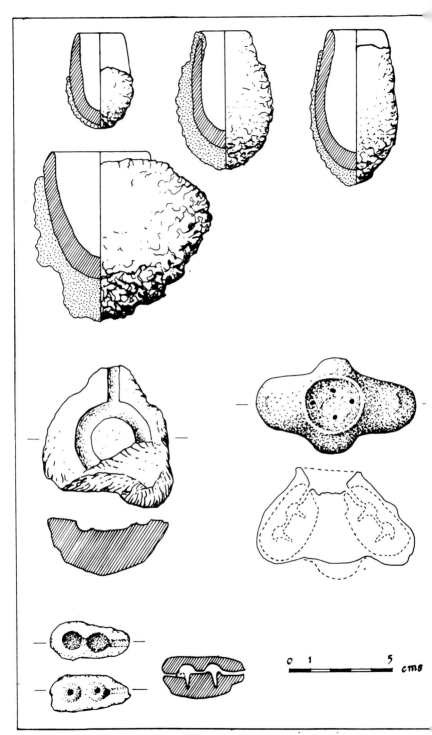

46. Crucibles and moulds at the Harpham villa

Other industries

There is surprisingly little evidence for other industries. At York there is evidence for the working of jet and bone into a variety of small useful or decorative objects. There is no evidence for the manufacture of jet objects on Parisian territory as there is on rural sites nearer Whitby. The main road route from Whitby, the source of the raw material, made for York and not for Malton. Bone objects probably were worked locally but evidence of the kind that has come from York has not been found. Carpentry and woodworking was another craft which probably had a local base but has not left very much trace in our area.

Buildings tend to be made from the best available local stone even where this was such a poor quality stone as chalk. There is some use of local sandstones from the coast north of Filey, but the best useable building stone is the oolitic limestone from the western edge of the Wolds and from the Malton area. This is not a particularly good building stone, but some was, exported to York. There, the better class magnesian limestone from west of Tadcaster or the Pennine gritstones were preferred. A built-up tomb or cist in rubble oolitic limestone was found at Trentholme Drive[35] and the same stone was used as an ingredient in mortar or in the core of walls.[36]

6. The Late Fourth and Fifth Centuries

In the middle to late fourth century the Parisi had to face two set-backs. The first was the result of natural causes. The increased flooding of the later fourth century, by whatever mechanism it was caused, rendered the site of the *civitas* capital untenable, as well as water-logging many rural areas in the Hull valley and the Vale of York. The evidence from York,[1] Brough[2] and Faxfleet[3] has been published. It is easy to overestimate the impact of the flooding, and as a corrective it is worth noticing the evidence from Drax,[4] which continued well into the later half of the fourth century on a site by the Ouse which must have suffered from the first flooding. There was probably a gradual build-up over the years of at first sporadic and then more frequent flooding, perhaps accentuated by the destruction of *Ocellum promontorium*, the Roman Spurn Point, in one of the cyclical changes that affect that peninsula. This flooding resulted in the deposition of silts, blocking harbours, roads, and communications generally and, perhaps more important, blocking the outlets to drainage and gradually waterlogging the land. A town like Brough, in addition to being affected by the periodical flooding of part of its walled area,[5] also lost its economic basis. Harbours at York,[6] Brough[7] and Faxfleet[8] silted up. Navigation in the Ouse and Humber, always difficult because of shifting shoals,[9] became even more so. With the silting of the harbour at Brough the Humber ferry was probably moved back to Ferriby. Even so ebb currents and high tides must have made it difficult and there must have been many hold-ups whilst passengers waited for a safe crossing. The other road from

Lincoln to York became the more attractive route and the southern part of the territory of the Parisi, which had formerly stood at a cross-roads, now became somewhat of a backwater. Settlement at Brough itself in the later fourth century was limited to one small corner.

The appearance at Malton at the same time of a unit with a name connecting it with *Petuaria* implies that some of the inhabitants of the town were drafted into the army and resettled at Malton. No doubt these were drawn from the strong artisan element whose existence at Brough is implied by the industrial sites within the walled area. The wealthier classes probably remained in their villas, for although decurions were compelled by legislation to live in cities, the very need for such legislation implied that they preferred not to. Brough does not seem to have contained houses fit for decurions to live in, at any rate none has yet been found. The villas to the north were near enough for their owners to be readily available for any duties. Wenham[10] has argued that the *civitas* capital was also moved to Malton on the assumption that a new town was laid out on the Norton side of the river, but the evidence for such a town will not bear scrutiny. That the centre of the *civitas* remained at the south end of their territory is implied by other evidence. Recent publication of, and reappraisal of the evidence from, the Germanic cremation cemetery at Sancton,[11] has revealed the early date of some of the burials in that cemetery, the earliest in this area outside York. If these, as Myres[12] has suggested, belong to *laeti* or mercenaries introduced during the late Roman period, the siting of the cemetery requires explanation. With Brough no longer a town after *c.* 350, and none of the military traffic which Myres postulates to and fro between Malton and Brough for the *laeti* to protect, Sancton is only explicable if the centre of the *civitas* remained somewhere north of Brough, perhaps under one of the villages.

The other setback that affected the Parisi was the concerted attack on the province by the Franks and Saxons from the east and the Atecotti and Scoti from the west in A.D. 367-9. How much the Parisi were affected by these attacks is better judged by the countermeasures adopted afterwards than by the necessarily incomplete and ambiguous archaeological record.

The Yorkshire coast, inhospitable as it was, lay beyond the defensive system of Saxon Shore forts and was an obvious target for raiders wishing to outflank that system. Count Theodosius' answer was to install a line of signal towers to keep watch along the coast, to alert the Roman navy, and to pass a message back if necessary to Malton where the *numerus supervenientium Petuariensium,* or the 'Anticipators' as Morris[13] translates *supervenientium,* could ride out and deal with any raiders that landed. But it is more probable that the purpose of the towers was to co-ordinate and control naval patrols rather than to act as warning beacons to landward. Malton was more of a service base for some of the stations than an integral part of a signalling system. The sites of five of the towers are known between Flamborough Head and the mouth of the Tees, and there were probably others extending the line. They occupy high headlands (fig. 47) and contained towers which may have risen to a considerable height, 90 or 100 ft. has been suggested.[14] The towers were built to a standard pattern but most is known about that at Goldsborough, about half a mile from the sea at Kettleness, at about 130 m. above sea level (fig. 48). A square with rounded corners, 52 m. across, was surrounded by a ditch, and set back within the ditch some ten metres was a defensive wall 1.2 m. thick at its base, with rounded corners strengthened by circular bastions or turrets. A south-facing gate gave access to an inner area, 32 m. square, of which the central feature was the tower, whose foundations, 1.7 m. thick, alone survived. That this building was a tower we know not only from the massiveness of its foundations but from an inscription from the next tower to the south at Ravenscar which refers to the construction of both tower and fort, *turrem et castrum,*[15] an apt description of the signal towers with their enclosures. The lowest apartment in the tower had its roof supported on posts set in stone sockets and the whole superstructure may have been in timber rather than stone. Water was supplied by a well within the enclosure. Founded *c.* A.D. 370, we do not know how long the towers remained in use. Pottery, entirely of the type which takes its name from them, does not enable us to fix the final date of their abandonment. The coin list goes on to Honorius; the paucity of later coins might imply that they did not survive

47. Site of the signal station at Filey

long after A.D. 400. But we do not know the significance of the
fading coin list, since we cannot be sure of the status of the last
occupants of the towers, whose bodies were found in the wells
and fireblackened ruins at Goldsborough and Huntcliff. These
bodies included those of men, women and children, not just
taking refuge there on the last day but living there as the finds
of spindle whorls and bangles tell us. Bones of pigs, oxen,
goats and deer, hares, rabbits, small birds and fish, shells of
crabs, mussels, limpets, whelks and periwinkles littered the
floor. Taken together with the querns they give us a clear idea
of the diet of the occupants. The bodies of dogs suggest that
they helped to hunt. The general picture is one of peasant
domesticity rather than of the life of a military detachment.
Such was the army of the late fourth century that we would be
hard put to say whether these last occupants were manning
the towers or squatting in a convenient home.

The bodies at Huntcliff were thrown into the well, as were

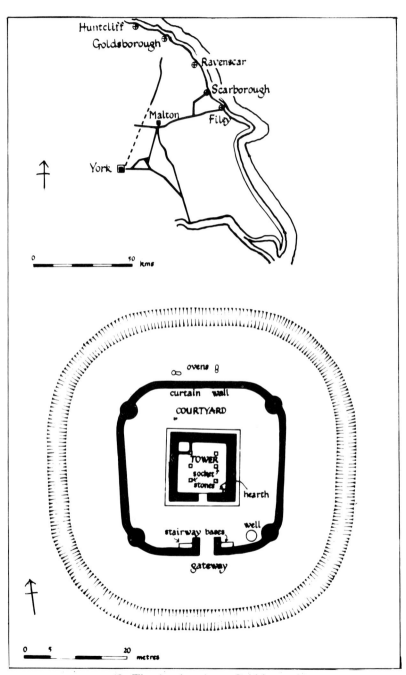

48. The signal station at Goldsborough

three of those at Goldsborough, but two others there give us a vivid picture of what happened on the last day even if we do not know when it was. In the ruins of the tower there lay the body of a short thick-set man fallen across the smouldering fire on an open hearth, perhaps stabbed in the back, face down, left hand behind his back with ring on his finger, right hand touching the wall. At his feet lay a taller man, also face down, fallen across the body of a large and powerful dog, head at the man's throat, paws on his shoulders. The dog had defended to the last, and not without a victim.

The inscription already referred to from the tower at Ravenscar, with its jumbled and poorly formed letters, is in sad contrast with earlier building inscriptions of the Roman army, and implies a considerable lowering of standards, one which is noticeable in other respects and other places. The signal stations were not the only military sites where peasant domesticity rather than military discipline was the order of the day. Frere[16] has listed succinctly the evidence from the Wall for a general lowering of standards in the Theodosian period, poor building techniques and the abandonment of the regular planning of earlier periods. Headquarters buildings were converted to store-houses and living quarters, and even granaries were given over to domestic purposes. Above all there is evidence for women and children living inside the forts. Richmond[17] describes garrisons of farmer-soldiers living with their women and children entirely within the forts, and receiving land to cultivate in return for their services.

At Malton[18] the women and children had moved into the fort before A.D. 367, where twenty-nine infant burials belong to an earlier date. Perhaps the change took place here with the introduction of the troops from *Petuaria*, who could have been here as early as A.D. 350. If so they must have suffered severely in the disaster of 367 when both fort and *vicus* were destroyed. The subsequent reconstruction within the fort bears the hallmark of Theodosian work – shoddiness. The north-eastern defences had been pretty well destroyed in A.D. 367-9. A temporary repair of the damaged gate was effected by a timber and earth barrier reducing its width to a mere 2.7 m. The wall was not rebuilt but replaced by earthwork defences, presumably with a timber stockade. A wide ditch was cut, partly on the old berm, partly through the wall foundations, up to 2.7 m. wide and 3.7 m. deep below the present ground surface. It had originally been intended to build the gate again on approximately its old position, since the gap in the new ditch implies this, but in the end, although the new gate reused the remnant of the south guard house, a new north guard house was built narrowing the gate towards the south and making it asymmetrical to the opening through the ditch. Crambeck and Huntcliff-type pottery left no doubt about the date of these repairs. In the last Roman phase of the fort's existence no surviving part of the masonry of any of the previous gates can have been visible above ground since all was covered with a mass of debris. The gate was merely a depression in the rampart bank, through which ran a lightly made metalled road, clearly showing the ruts of wheeled traffic. It is separated by 0.5 m. of rubbish from the Theodosian roadway. At some later period an emergency measure was taken to protect this entrance into the fort. A deep vertical-sided trench or ditch was dug across the front of the entrance and another 12.8 m. in advance. It is very difficult to fix a time scale for all this, but some while must be assumed to have elapsed before the Theodosian repairs to the gate were allowed to fall into disuse, and more time to have passed while the inhabitants of the fort rutted the road in peace before the final emergency defence was needed, perhaps well into the fifth century. A fifth-century long brooch comes from the fort and in 1976 a cruciform Anglian brooch was brought into the museum from plough soil between the fort and Old Malton.

The *vicus* at Malton also was laid waste in 367 and much of it was not rebuilt.[19] Wacher refers to the virtual abandonment of the *vicus* for the safety provided by the fort,[20] so that it must have ended its life more like a walled town. But although some of the *vicus* appears to have been abandoned Wenham claims to have found both Theodosian and later structures in his excavations in 1968-70.[21] A late defensive ditch was ruthlessly cut through earlier fourth-century buildings from the south-east gate to the river, with a rampart on its south-west side surmounted by a palisade. As some of Wenham's Theodosian buildings lie outside these defences they probably belong to a later phase and are not to be equated with the earth and timber defence on the north-east side of the fort. They represent a later stage when the *vicus* had shrunk towards the river bridge. There is a continuing decline also in the standard of buildings, even below the Theodosian.

It is not clear when the Roman site was deserted in favour of Old Malton. There is some evidence to suggest that this was already the main seat of occupation by the seventh to eighth centuries. The siting of the late defences and the destruction in 367-9 suggest that it was from the north-east direction that trouble came and the English may have found that site easier to occupy than the defended site at Malton. Urns from Broughton, west of Malton, in the Yorkshire Museum have been cited[22] as the burials of *laeti*, barbarians brought in with their wives and families and deliberately planted to act as a reinforcement or substitute for more regular garrisons, but doubt has been cast on the provenance of these urns.[23] Nevertheless Anglian finds were certainly made at Broughton[24] even if they cannot now be identified in the Yorkshire Museum.

Among the villas Langton is usually cited as an example of one that suffered at the hands of raiders in the events following 367-9, and it is possible that they passed this way after the sack of Malton, pressing down the York road but finding time to take the side road to the villa. But the evidence posed by Corder[24] is not substantial enough for us to be sure. The villa certainly survived the attack, if there was one, and its economy flourished. Crambeck and Huntcliff-type pottery is there in quantity. More than that, there is a considerable number of coins from the last decade of the fourth century. Langton is one of the few villas where a money economy was active at the opening of the fifth century. How did Langton end? The answer was found in the well. Constructed or last cleaned out soon after A.D. 335, when a coin in mint condition was dropped into the well right to the bottom, it had then been filled up, and the pottery in that filling shows that it had remained in use, if only as a rubbish dump, to the end of the occupation of the villa. It had been filled to a depth of some 6 m. below the top. Above this was a sticky black layer containing quantities of charcoal and decayed vegetable matter. Corder considered this layer to have accumulated gradually by seepage from a deserted site. It is from the level below this that the ox bones come which Applebaum considered to have belonged to the last ox-team used on the site. Above the black level the well has a deliberate fill which Corder suggests derives from clearance of the site for ploughing. The building stone in the well shows clear signs of burning and Corder is right in saying that the villa ended in a conflagration. The date at which this happened may have been well into the fifth century. The English village that succeeded to its boundaries was on a new site, less exposed and nearer to running water but not very far from the site of the western house on the estate.

Among the finds from Langton was a bone comb (fig. 49) decorated with confronted animals and bone circles, features of an art style current at the end of the fourth century and early in the fifth. The style is common on bronze belt fittings[25] and there is a fine example of such a one from Catterick[26] in the territory of the Brigantes. Another similar comb comes from the Beadlam villa,[27] as also does a bronze strap-end with a chip carved design of a type well known from late Roman and Dark Age contexts (fig. 49). The coin list from Beadlam repeats the evidence from Langton and shows that this villa too was flourishing at the beginning of the fifth century. The thinning out of the coin list at Malton at the end of the fourth century corresponds with the decline of other standards there and reflects a growing poverty in comparison with the villas.

If we see the villas entering the fifth century in prosperity, while Malton declines into a second-rate urban community – a walled slum, but still worth defending, even if in doing so it cuts off its communication to the north-east and never opens it again – we cannot but ask what happened to the potteries at Crambeck. Clearly the kilns must still have been producing when the villa at Langton came to an end. It is hard to believe the filling of the well there to be anything but deliberate; it must mark the end of the occupation of that site. Considerable Crambeck pottery was included in that fill. The potteries probably went on producing into the fifth century, though on a declining scale, even after their widespread northern distribution had ceased. At Crambeck Corder found two

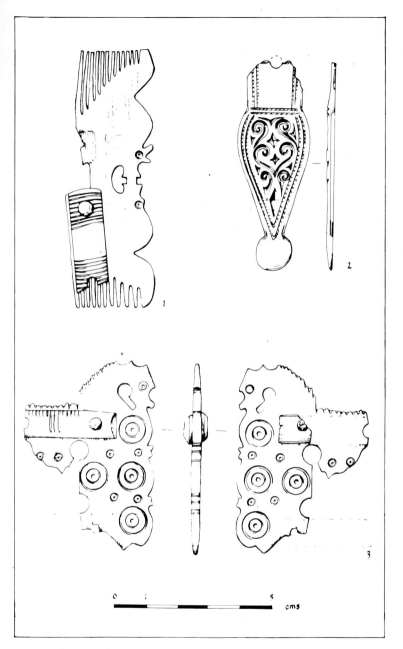

49. Late fourth-century finds from Langton (1) and Beadlam (2, 3).

inhumation burials in cists, with slabs of local limestone set upright and cover slabs over. This type of burial was a local feature both of the Howardian Hills and the limestone hills north of the Vale of Pickering.[28] It occurs in the fourth century and survives into the Anglian period. Cist burial is not an Anglo-Saxon rite and its survival implies continuity. The cists at Crambeck overlay kilns which Corder estimated must have been abandoned some 30 years before the construction of the cists. Pots were buried with the bodies. With one was a squat grey spherical vessel with outflaring rim in Crambeck ware and technique in a form evolved from other fourth-century types though unparalleled from Crambeck. With the other was a unique vessel, a tumbler in a hard blue-grey ware externally burnished, ornamented with a series of grooves round the girth of the pot.[29] The kilns excavated by Corder lie towards the edge of the kiln field some distance from the potters' earth deposits by the Cram Beck, and therefore belong to the period of the greatest expansion of the kilns after A.D. 367. Thirty years later would bring these graves into the fifth century, and perhaps well into that century. Other kilns were then still working, although producing anomalous products.

When we turn to the more vulnerable eastern part of the territory, the evidence is not so clear. We must await the full publication of the evidence from Rudston, but on the basis of the earlier published coin list which ends with Gratian (A.D. 367-383), there does not seem to be the same preponderance of late coins as at Langton and they finish earlier. But on the other hand there is some evidence for what was happening on smaller rural sites. Elmswell near Driffield lies, as the place name implies, near springs which must have attracted settlement at any time, so that the fact that the same site produces Huntcliff-type wares, indicating occupation certainly in the late fourth century and possibly into the fifth as well as Anglian pottery, a comb and a cruciform brooch of the sixth century, need not imply continuity of occupation. But in an Anglian inhumation cemetery about a kilometre to the west there is evidence of the survival of burial customs, as there was in the limestone hills, but here with a difference. Whereas in the limestone hills the cist burials represent the continuance of a late Roman burial custom, here it is a pre-Roman one that survives. The Anglo-Saxon cemetery lies in the north ditch of a double dyke on the south boundary of Garton parish. A long barrow incorporated in the bank of the dyke whose ditches curve round it serves as a marker to divide the cemetery into two. To the east the burials are aligned carefully east to west, coffined without grave goods and probably Christian. To the west, the burials are aligned with the ditch, normally uncoffined, and many with grave goods. Amongst these occur some contracted burials with joints of meat, a pre-Roman and not an Anglian custom. Another cemetery lies on the northern boundary of Garton,[30] with the burials this time in the bank and not the ditch of a dyke. This cemetery included late burials, one with a purse of coins dated A.D. 740-50. Only one burial was contracted here, but it was exceptional in another way also; it was the only grave to cut through another one, demonstrating that it was not a burial from an earlier period.

Elmswell was not the only site of native type to be occupied or reoccupied in the sixth century. The well-known site at Wykeham, west of Scarborough overlapped with a settlement producing late fourth-century pottery.[32] Crossgates, Seamer[33] was the site of a Langton type farm in the first century but did not develop like Langton into a villa. By the early second century occupation had spread outside the enclosure where two floors were excavated. There is then a gap in the pottery sequence from the site from about A.D. 120 to the middle of the third century. Well built round huts with stone foundations belonged to the late fourth century on the evidence of the considerable quantity of Crambeck and Huntcliff-type pottery that was found. Coins were scarce but included one of Valens (364-78). Iron slag was found and a small furnace fired by brown coal or lignite. Analysis of the charcoal did not produce sufficient evidence to say whether the furnace was used for smelting, smithing or for a corn drier. There were a large number of querns from the site and the economy was probably a mixed one. Bones from the site implied the rearing of cattle, sheep and pigs. The sequence from fourth-century Romano-British to sixth-century Anglian is not clear. We do not know how late, if at all, the Roman site survived into the fifth century, and the coins are too few to help. The Anglian structures do not overlap onto the Roman but lie distinct to the west. Some fourth century Roman pottery was found on the Anglian site. Structures consisted of what the excavators diagnosed as open-air hearths and two sunken hut floors with internal hearths. It is impossible to prove whether there was a gap in the occupation as there had been in the second to third centuries or whether one similar farm had developed from the other.

Staxton[34] shows similar gaps in occupation, but more clearly discernible in that the slow filling up of one of the ditches has interleaved the occupation levels with barren layers. There is no occupation between the early second century and the late occupation, which consists mainly of sixth-century pottery. The ditch is at the fringe of the occupation however, and air photography shows a further native farm a little to the south. Among the Anglian pottery was a fourth-century Marne bowl and metal-work identified by the excavator as fifth century. More certainly fifth-century are two brooches in Hull Museum rescued from the adjacent quarry. At Elmswell, Seamer, Staxton and Wykeham there is sixth-century occupation or reoccupation of native farmsteads where fourth-century occupation may or may not have continued into the fifth. Another similar site occurs at Bessingby near Bridlington,[35] a small Romano-British farmstead with a rectangular hut floor and late fourth-century pottery and a coin of Valentinian I (364-75) but no following Anglian occupation. If there is any continuity in the north-eastern part of the Parisian territory it is probably among the native farms, and cultural survivals are native rather than Roman.

In the south the only villas for which evidence is available are Welton and Brantingham. Welton continued late, with occupation until at least A.D. 400. Brantingham, less integrated into the countryside, and more closely associated with South Humberside, seems to have ended its occupation at the same time as the main occupation at Brough. Rigby,[36] discussing the pottery from the villa, finds a significant absence of the Crambeck forms which are characteristic of middle to late fourth century groups in northern England and of Huntcliff-type cooking pots, and dates the pottery no later than the first half of the fourth century.

It is from this area that we have our earliest evidence at Sancton for the presence of Germanic settlers, and at Brough, as one might expect at a port in touch with the continent, even earlier evidence of the import of Germanic pottery. A jar stratified with normal Romano-British pottery of *c.* 300 had its nearest parallels in proto-Anglian pottery.[37] The first users of the cemetery at Sancton,[38] which is situated just to the west of the Roman road to Malton 13.5 km. north of Brough, comprised people of both Anglian and Saxon origin, and both elements, if the dates of continental parallels to their pottery can be accepted, are likely to have been present before the collapse of the Roman authority in the opening years of the fifth century. They must have come as allies, *laeti*, settled by the Romans with their wives and families to defend the Parisi. But having come they were reinforced during the fifth century in strength, perhaps at the wish of the Romans, perhaps uninvited. The newcomers came from the same areas of the continent as before, but now also included people of mixed Anglo-Saxon and Frisian origin. There are also cultural links with south and central Germany, an interesting fact in view of the preservation as an heirloom of a fourth-century Alamannic brooch by someone who was buried in the cemetery at Londesborough, 7.5 km. further along the road to Malton, in the sixth century.[39] Myres has outlined a case for Alamannic *laeti* in fourth century Yorkshire.[40]

Thus, as we have seen, the evidence for the transition from the Romano-British Parisi to the English of Deira is fragile. Some slight record there may be, in the reference in a Northumbrian genealogy to Soemil who first separated Deira from Bernicia.[41] Soemil,.the great-great-great-grandfather of Edwin, should have lived in the second half of the fifth century and may have been responsible for detaching East Yorkshire from the command at York – if, as Morris suggests, there was still a functioning command there –[42] and setting up his own independent kingdom. The archaeological record includes evidence for destruction and evidence for survival. Roman culture seems to have survived longest around Malton and in the limestone hills. Native traditions and peasant farms survived longest in the east. In the south, English who came first as defenders settled then in strength with the success of cuckoos in the nest.

Notes and references

References to British journals use the abbreviations recommended by the Council for British Archaeology, which are those of the American Standards Association (list Z39, 5-1963, revised 1966). Other abbreviations used are:

OS   Ordnance Survey
RCHM   Royal Commission on Historical Monuments (England)
RIB   R.G. Collingwood and R.P. Wright *Roman Inscriptions of Britain* i (Oxford 1965)
VCH   *Victoria County History*

Many unreferenced sites and references to fieldwork by RCHM will be published in the following future Inventories of RCHM:
Archaeological Sites, East Riding of Yorkshire, i and ii
Roman Military Sites in the North of England, i and ii

1. TRIBAL TERRITORY AND THE PRE-ROMAN IRON AGE

1. Marshall *1788* i, 146ff. For general descriptions of the topography of East Yorkshire see Boer *1965* and Harris *1961* and the map of farming regions in Marshall, W., *The review and abstract of the county reports to the Board of Agriculture: i, The Northern Department* (York 1818).
2. Ramm *1971*, 181-3. Radley and Simms *1970*, 9. For a general description of the nature of the Ouse see Duckham *1967*, 9ff.
3. Buckland and Kenwood *1973*; Challis and Harding *1975* i, 8-9.
4. Radley and Simms *1970*, 8 and fig. 1.
5. Varley *1968*.
6. Stead *1971a*, 21.
7. Wacher *1969*, 4.
8. Sheppard, T., *The Lost Towns of the Yorkshire Coast* (London 1912); Sheppard, J., *1966*, 6; Boer *1965*, 208-9.
9. Brooks, F.W., *The Battle of Stamford Bridge, East Yorkshire Local History Series*, no. 6 (York 1963).
10. Ramm *1966*.
11. Harris *1961*, 31-2.
12. Morris, J.E., *The East Riding of Yorkshire* (London 1906) 9.

13. Mortimer *1905*, 152.
14. e.g. the gazetteer published by Clark *1935*.
15. Manby, T.G., 'Neolithic occupation sites in the Yorkshire Wolds', *Yorkshire Archaeol. J.* xlvii (1975), 23.
16. Turner, J., 'Post-Neolithic disturbance of British vegetation', in Walker and West (eds.), *Studies in the vegetational history of the British Isles, Essays in honour of Harry Godwin* (1970), 17-18.
17. Dunn *1976*
18. Brewster *1976*, 107.
19. McInnes *1968*. The arrangement of the burials outside the ring ditch suggests that there may have been an external bank.
20. Wainwright and Longworth *1969*.
21. Varley *1968*.
22. Stead *1968*.
23. Challis and Harding *1975* i, 33.
24. Dept. of Environment, *Archaeological Excavations 1973*, 31, *1974*, 28.
25. Challis and Harding *1975* i, 122.
26. Brewster *1963*.
27. Smith *1927*; Wheeler *1931*, 20ff.
28. Challis and Harding *1975* ii, fig. 86.
29. O.S. Records, TA 15 NW2. Pottery: Brewster *1963*, 141; Challis and Harding *1975* i, 57.
30. Brewster *1976*.
31. Stead *1961*, *1965*, *1971a*.
32. Sheppard *1938*, 35.
33. Challis and Harding *1975* i, 167. Rillington: Harding, D.W., *The Iron Age in Lowland Britain* (London 1974), plate xx.
34. Challis and Harding *1975* i, 187.
35. Challis and Harding *1975* i, 172-3.
36. Stead *1971a*, 23.
37. Stead *1971a*, 324.
38. St. Joseph, J.K., 'Air reconnaissance: recent results', 23, *Antiquity*, xlx (1971), 48.
39. Piggot *1958*, 14.
40. Stead *1965*, 78-80.
41. *Geographia* II, 3, 10.
42. *RIB* 707.
43. Richmond *1954a*, 44.
44. Boer *1965*, 210, *1964*; Sheppard *1966*, 7ff.
45. *Britannia Romana* 374.
46. Hinderwell, T., *History and Antiquities of Scarborough* (York, 2nd. ed., 1811), 276.
47. Sheppard *1913*, 46.
48. Tees: Richmond *1954b*, 61. Scarborough: Stead *1965*, 71, 79.
49. Jackson *1948*, 57.
50. Jackson *1948*, 57, *1970*, 72; Richmond and Crawford *1949*, 32.
51. Richmond and Crawford *1949*, 31. Petrucorii: Frere *1961*, 35.
52. Challis and Harding *1975* ii, figs. 82 and 83.

2. HISTORY: A.D. 43-367.

1. Frere *1974*, 71; Piggott *1958*, 13ff.; Rivet *1958*, 71.
2. Riley *1973*, 210; *1974*, 157; *1975*, 13.
3. Although superficially the earthworks at Barwick-in-Elmet are those of the motte and bailey castle, fieldwork by RCHM and observation of building trenches have shown that a hill-fort has been adapted for use as a motte and bailey castle by the same Norman magnate who also adapted the hill-fort at Almondbury. Certain anomalous features of the works as a motte and bailey become readily explicable on the assumption of adaptation from an earlier hill-fort.
4. Hartley *1971*, 56. The square barrows near York are to be published shortly by H.G. Ramm.
5. Tacitus, *Ann*. xii, 32.
6. Allen *1963*, 22ff.
7. Wheeler *1954*.
8. Tacitus, *Ann*. xii, 40.
9. Tacitus, *Hist*. iii, 45.
10. Statius, *Silvae* v, ii, 145-6. Birley *1953*, 13 followed by Wenham *1971*, 47.
11. Richmond *1955*, 37.
12. Frere *1974*, 138.
13. Simpson *1973*, 84. There is no doubt about the Neronian pottery. The difficulty lies with the association of the datable objects with the three forts. 'Any attempt to date Templeborough's forts will always be hypothetical' (Simpson, *loc. cit.*) Having said this, however, Simpson agreed with both May and Frere (*1974*, 101) in ascribing the founding of Templeborough to Didius Gallus, governor, A.D. 52-57, but after A.D. 54, quoting early Neronian parallels to the samian from Trent Vale, Stoke-on-Trent. Fewer assumptions are made in supposing that the earliest finds belong to the earliest known fort than in assuming an unknown site to underlie it.
14. Todd *1973*, 31. Jones *1975*, 176. *J. Roman. Stud.* lix (1969), 164.
15. Hartley *1971*, 56.
16. Riley *1973*, 213.
17. Wheeler *1954*, 21.
18. Frere *1974*, 138.
19. Tacitus *Agricola*, 17.
20. Wacher *1969*.
21. Frere *1974*, 117.
22. Stead *1977*; *J. Roman Stud.* lv (1965), 202; Jones *1975*, 184.
23. By S. Johnson. A report is to be published in *Britannia*, which will also contain plans of the native sites based on air-photographic interpretation by RCHM.
24. Ramm *1955*.
25. Ramm *1966*.
26. Corder *1930*, 64.
27. Frere *1974*, 117.
28. Wenham *1974*, 9, 12, and 13.

29. Wenham *1974*, 12. The resemblance in fact is to the defences found by
    Corder and Romans (*1939*, 184-94) which Wacher (*1969*, 8) proved to
    be the annexe defences of the first Flavian fort at Brough and not of the
    Flavian temporary camp. Wenham confirms that the dimensions given
    in Wenham, *1974*, 12 are correct and not the much larger and different
    sets of measurements given in *Britannia* ii (1971), 253, and Jones *1975*,
    164 both relying on information from Wenham.
30. Rodwell *1975*, 85. For the aqueduct see chapter 4.
31. Hartley *1971*, 58.
32. For previous excavation: Hayes and Rutter *1964*, 69ff. Excavation
    August 1976 by B.R. Hartley.
33. Corder and Kirk *1932*, 26-33; Richmond *1932*; Goodall *1969*, 8.
34. *J. Roman Stud.* lvi (1966), 199; Goodall *1969*, 8.
35. Rutter and Duke *1958*, 10ff; Goodall *1969*, 9.
36. Ramm *1976a*, 10. Bradford *1957*, 211-16. See chapter 4.
37. Hartley *1971*, 60.
38. Wacher *1969*, 3.
39. *Britannia* ii (1971), 291; Wenham *1974*, 34 and plate 1.
40. Richmond *1933*, 46.
41. *RIB* 707.
42. Wacher *1974*, 395-7.
43. Wacher *1969*, 23 n.4 for references for the contrversy; Frere *1961*.
44. *RIB* 707.
45. Birley, E.B., 'The inscribed stone', in Corder and Romans *1939*, 229-32.
46. Hartley *1971*, 62 and 67 n.54.
47. Wenham *1974*, 16.
48. Smith *1969*, 102; Liversidge, Smith and Stead *1973*, 78-9; Smith *1976*,
    28; Stead *1977*.
49. Todd *1973*, 42-4.
50. Wacher *1969, passim; 1971*, 176; *1974*, 393ff.
51. Frere *1974*, 403.
52. Corder *1930*, 47.
53. Wacher *1969*, 54, 74; *1971*, 175.

3. COMMUNICATIONS AND URBAN SETTLEMENT

1. Horace, *Satires* i, 5.
2. Wacher *1974*, 166. For the text *J. Roman Stud.* xi (1921), 107. For the
   Ouse navigation see Duckham *1967*.
3. *RLB* 653. RCHM *1962*, 116, no. 36.
4. Richmond *1947*, 67.
5. Richmond *1955*, 179.
6. Harden, D.B., 'Glass in Roman York', in RCHM 1962, 136.
7. RCHM *1962*, 141-2. Richmond *1966*, 83.
8. Richmond *1966*, 84.
9. Todd *1973*, 47.
10. Ramm *1972*, ix-x.

11. Reader *1972*, 2-4.
12. Corder and Richmond *1942*, 32.
13. Wacher *1969*, 26.
14. Ramm *1971*, 187-8.
15. In RCHM, *1962*, xxix.
16. North, F.J., 'Geology for archaeologists', *Archaeol. J.* xciv (1934), 73.
17. Cole *1899*.
18. Clark *1935*, 32ff.
19. Margary *1967*.
20. *Rep. Yorkshire Philosophical Soc. for 1975* (1976), 34.
21. Ramm *1955*.
22. Wenham *1974*, 14.
23. Richmond and Crawford *1949*, 2ff.
24. Rodwell *1975*, 86.
25. OS *Map of Roman Britain* (3rd ed., Chessington, 1956).
26. Richmond and Crawford *1949*, 31.
27. Wacher *1969*, 26; Rodwell *1975*, 84.
28. Rivet *1970*, 41n.
29. Jackson *1970*, 72.
30. Smith, A.H., *The Place-names of the East Riding of Yorkshire and York* (Cambridge 1937), 3.
31. *RIB* 707.
32. Wacher *1974*, 393ff.
33. See chapter 5.
34. Wacher *1974*, 397.
35. Wacher *1969*, 73.
36. Wenham *1974*, 39 and fig. 13.
37. Mitchelson *1964*, 235.
38. In conversation with the writer.
39. Mitchelson *1964*.
40. *Britannia* i (1970), 280; ii (1971), 252.
41. Wenham *1974*, 35ff.
42. *RIB* 712.
43. *RIB* 714.
44. *RIB* 713.
45. *RIB* 711.

4. RURAL SETTLEMENT

1. Ramm *1976a*, 10-11.
2. Corder and Kirk *1932*.
3. Richmond *1932*.
4. Webster *1969*, 246.
5. Corder and Kirk *1932*, 30ff. and fig. 7.
6. Stead *1968*, 172 fig. 16.
7. Clark *1935*, 97-8.
8. Rutter and Duke *1958*, 10ff.

9. *J. Roman Stud.* lvi (1966), 199; *Britannia* ii (1971), 253; Goodall *1969*, 9.
10. e.g. Webster, G., *The Cornovii* (London 1975), 92, fig. 39.
11. Dept. of Environment, *Archaeological Excavations 1971*, 24.
12. Brewster *1957*.
13. Corder *1940*; Corder and Hawkes *1940*; Fox *1958*, 105-6.
14. Webster *1969*, 247.
15. Clark *1935*, 97.
16. Applebaum *1972*, 173.
17. Webster *1969*, 247.
18. Applebaum *1972*, 119.
19. Webster *1969*, 247.
20. RCHM *1962*, 53 no. 27, pl. 23.
21. *RIB* 720.
22. Ramm *1971*, 191.
23. Clark *1935*, 88.
24. Wenham *1960*, 298; *J. Roman Stud.* xlvii (1957), 228.
25. Biró, M., 'The inscriptions of Roman Britain', *Acta Archaeologica Academiae Scientiarum Hungaricae*, xxvii (1953), 13.
26. Clark, *1935*, 111, 123; Goodall *1969*, 37.
27. Clark *1935*, 88; Goodall *1969*, 35.
28. Clark *1935*, 119; Goodall *1969*, 35.
29. Stead *1971b*, 178.
30. Clark *1935*, 85; *Yorkshire Archaeol. J.* xliii (1971), 194.
31. Woodward *1934*, *1935*; Woodward and Steer *1936*.
32. *J. Roman Stud.* liii (1963), 130; liv (1964), 157; lv (1965), 204; lvi (1966), 199; lvii (1967), 179. *Britannia* ii (1971) 253; iv (1973), 281; v (1974), 310. The report will be published by Dr. Stead as a Yorkshire Archaeological Society monograph.
33. Smith *1976*, 5ff.
34. Sheppard *1905*; Collier *1907*; Mellor *1950*, *1952*; Goodall *1969*, 27.
35. Gent, T., *The Ancient and Modern History of Ripon* (York 1733), 77, quoted Clark *1935*, 67.
36. Liversidge, Smith and Stead *1973*.
37. Smith *1969*, 102; Liversidge, Smith and Stead *1973*, 78-9; Smith *1976*, 28.
38. *Britannia* iii (1972), 311; iv (1973), 281; v (1974), 414; vi (1975), 237. Wilson, D.R., 'Romano-British villas from the air,' *Britannia* v (1974), 251.
39. South Cave: Clark *1935*, 74; *Yorkshire Archaeol. J.* xliv (1972), 220. North Cave: *Yorkshire Archaeol. J.* xlvii (1975), 4. Newbald, south site: Corder *1941*, who called the site North Newbald although it lay south-west of South Newbald. Newbald, north site: *Yorkshire Archaeol. J.* xxxix (1958), 335, where the site is unfortunately called South Newbald although it lies north of North Newbald. Nunburnholme: Morris, M.C.F., *Nunburnholme* (Oxford 1907), 15-16, 149-50.
40. Ms. addition to Drake *1736*, 32-3; Clark *1935*, 109; plan: Haynes *1744*.
41. Todd *1973*, 84-5, fig. 19.
42. Rutter and Duke *1958*, 15ff.

43. Ms. addition to Drake *1736*, 32.
44. Todd *1973*, 102-3, figs. 25 and 28.
46. Alcock, J., 'Celtic water cults in Roman Britain', *Archaeol. J.* cxxii (1965), 1.
47. Lewis, M.J.T., *Temples in Roman Britain* (Cambridge 1966), 86.
48. Stead *1971a*, 32; Brewster *1976*, 114, and fig. on 113.
49. Mortimer *1905*, 198, and plate lxiv, fig. 492.
50. Grantham Collection, Driffield.
51. Wenham *1974*, 6 and plate viii, fig. 14.
52. Stead, *1971a*, 34.
53. *Yorkshire Archaeol. J.* xxiv, 321; *Archaeol. Aeliana* xxxix, 75.
54. Marshall *1788* i, 147n.
55. Clark *1935*, 110.
56. Fieldwork and air-photographic interpretation by RCHM. Account of part in Mortimer *1905*, 383.

5. INDUSTRY AND THE ECONOMY

1. Todd *1973*, fig. 18.
2. Wenham *1974*, 14.
3. Applebaum *1972*, 114.
4. Applebaum *1972*, 173.
5. *De rust. re.* xii, 13.
6. Ramm, McDowall, and Mercer *1970*, 52, fig. 14; Brunskill, R.W., 'Vernacular architecture in the Northern Pennines', *Northern History* xi (1976), 130.
7. Frere *1974*, 259.
8. RCHM *1962*, 63 no. 48.
9. Corder *1930*, fig. 7.
10. In Butler *1971*, 137.
11. RCHM *1962*, 1, no. 1 and fig. 2.
12. Reader *1972*, 3.
13. Corder *1931*.
14. Clark *1935*, 88, Hicks and Wilson *1975*, 51.
15. Hicks and Wilson *1975*, 49.
16. Hicks and Wilson *1975*, 51.
17. Wacher *1969*, 134.
18. Lloyd *1968*.
19. Hayes and Whitley *1950*.
20. Wenham *1967*, 23.
21. Corder *1928*, Corder and Birley *1937*.
22. Corder *1928*, 12.
23. King and Moore *1975*.
24. Corder and Kirk *1932*, 96.
25. Clark *1935*, 63.
26. In Wenham *1968*, 64-8.
27. *Yorkshire Archaeol. J.* xli (1966), 323.

28. Ramm *1976b*,, 39, 68.
29. Manning, W.H., in Hicks and Wilson *1975*, 67ff.
30. Wacher *1969*, 227ff.
31. Corder *1930*, 28ff.
32. Corder *1940*.
33. Goodall *1969*, 47; *1972*.
34. Corder and Richmond *1942*, 32; Wacher *1969*, 25-6.
35. Wenham *1968*, 44.
36. RCHM *1962*, 10; *J. Roman Stud.* xlvi (1956), 89.

6. THE LATE FOURTH AND FIFTH CENTURIES

1. Ramm *1971*, 181.
2. Wacher *1969*, passim.
3. Ramm *1972*, x-xi.
4. Wilson, K., 'A survey and excavations within the area of Scurff Hall Farm, Drax, near Selby, Yorks', *Yorkshire Archaeol. J.* xli (1966), 680. Drax was abandoned after A.D. 370, although not necessarily very much later.
5. Wacher *1969*, 54.
6. Ramm *1971*, 181.
7. Wacher *1969*, 54.
8. Ramm *1972*, x-xi; Wacher *1969*, 54.
9. Wacher *1969*, 79; Duckham *1967*, 22, but the whole of chapter 1 is relevant.
10. Wenham *1974*, 39.
11. Myres and Southern *1973*.
12. Myres *1969*, 74.
13. Morris *1973*, 16.
14. Hornsby and Laverick *1932*, 209. For the signal stations generally see Collingwood *1931*; Elgee *1933*, 170ff. Huntcliff: Hornby and Stanton *1912*. Ravenscar: Clark *1935*, 121. Filey: Clark *1935*, 82.
15. *RIB* 721.
16. Frere *1974*, 403, n. 43.
17. Richmond *1955*, 63.
18. Corder *1931*, 67.
19. Mitchelson *1964*, 237.
20. Wacher *1971*, 175.
21. Wenham *1974*, 38
22. Blair *1947*.
23. Myres *1969*, 74n.
24. Corder and Kirk *1932*, 62.
25. Hawkes and Dunning *1961*, passim.
26. Hawkes and Dunning *1961*, 43, 62; Pocock *1971*, 187-8.
27. Stead *1971b*, 186.
28. Ramm *1971*, 191.
29. Corder *1928*, 19, 41, figs. 6, 7, 14, plate vii, nos. 192, 193.

30. South cemetery: Mortimer *1905*, 247-51. North cemetery: Mortimer *1905*, 355-60.
31. *Yorkshire Archaeol. J.* xli (1965), 355-60.
32. Moore *1965*.
33. Rutter and Duke *1958*.
34. Brewster *1957*, 200, 211, 218.
35. Hayes *1958*, 30; *Yorkshire Archaeol. J.* xxxvii (1951), 438-40, 523-4.
36. Liversidge, Smith and Stead *1973*, 106.
37. Wacher *1969*, 192-4.
38. Myres and Southern *1973*.
39. Swanton *1967*, but now see Todd, M., 'The "Alamannic" brooch from Londesborough, Yorks', *Antiq. J.* lv (1975), 384.
40. Myres *1969*, 75; Swanton *1967*, 45-50.
41. Blair *1947*, 43-4; Faull *1974*, 22-3.
42. Morris *1966*, 149; *1973*, 53-4.

Bibliography

Allen, D.F. (1963) *The Coins of the Coritani* (London).

Applebaum, S. (1972) 'Roman Britain', *in* Finberg, H.P.R. (ed.), *The Agrarian History of England and Wales* I-ii (Cambridge).

Birley, E.B. (1963) *Roman Britain and the Roman army* (Kendal).

Blair, P.H. (1947) 'The origins of Northumbria', *Archaeol. Aeliana* xxv, 1.

Boer, G. de (1964) 'Spurn Head and its evolution', *Trans. Inst. Brit. Geogr.* xxxiv, 71.

Boer, G. de (1965) 'Eastern Yorkshire: the geographical background to early settlement', *in* Small A. (ed.), *The Fourth Viking Congress, York August 1961*, Aberdeen University Studies, no. 149, 197.

Bradford, J. (1957) *Ancient Landscapes* (London).

Brewster, T.C.M. (1957) 'Excavations at Newham's Pit, Staxton, 1947-8', *Yorkshire Archaeol. J.* xxxix, 193.

Brewster, T.C.M. (1963) *The Excavation of Staple Howe* (Winteringham, Malton).

Brewster, T.C.M. (1976) 'Garton Slack', *Current Archaeol.* v, no. 51, 104.

Buckland, P.C. and Kenward, H.K. (1973) 'Thorne Moor: a palaeo-ecological study of a Bronze Age site', *Nature* ccxli (no. 5389 Feb. 9), 405.

Butler, R.M. (ed.) (1971) *Soldier and Civilian in Roman Yorkshire* (Leicester).

Challis, A.J. and Harding, D.W. (1975) *Later Prehistory from the Trent to the Tyne*, Brit. Archaeol. Reps. no. 20, i and ii (Oxford).

Clark, M.K. (1935) *A Gazeteer of Roman Remains in East Yorkshire*, Roman Malton and District Rep. no. 5. (Leeds).

Cole, E.M. (1899) 'Roman roads in the East Riding', *Trans. East Riding Antiq. Soc.* vii, 37.

Collier, C.V. (1907) 'The Roman remains at Harpham', *Trans. East Riding Antiq. Soc.* xiii, 141.

Collingwood, R.G. (1931) 'The Roman Signal Station', *in* Rowntree *1931*, 40.

Corder, P. (1928) *The Roman Pottery at Crambeck, Castle Howard*, Roman Malton and District Rep. no. 1 (York).

Corder, P. (1930) *The Defences of the Roman fort at Malton*, Roman Malton and District Rep. no. 2 (Malton).

Corder, P. (1931) 'The Roman pottery at Throlam, Holme-on-Spalding Moor, East Yorks', *Trans. East Riding Antiq. Soc.* xxvii, 6.

Corder, P. (1940) *Excavations at Elmswell, East Yorkshire, 1938* (Hull).

Corder, P. (1941) 'Roman site at North Newbald, East Yorkshire', *Proc. Leeds Philosoph. and Lit. Soc.* v, 231.

Corder, P. and Birley, M. (1937) 'Fourth century Romano-British Kilns near Crambeck', *Antiq. J.* xvii, 398.

Corder, P. and Hawkes, C.F.C. (1940) 'A panel of Celtic ornament from Elmswell, East Yorkshire', *Antiq. J.* xx, 338.

Corder, P. and Kirk, J.L. (1932) *A Roman villa at Langton, near Malton, E. Yorkshire, Roman Malton and District Rep. no. 5 (Leeds).*

Corder, P. and Richmond, I.A. (1942) 'Petuaria', *J. Brit. Archaeol. Assoc.* ser. 3, vii, 1.

Corder, P. and Romans, T. (1939) 'Excavations at Brough-Petuaria', *Trans. East Riding Antiq. Soc.* xxviii, 173.

Drake, F. (1736) *Eboracum, or the history and antiquities of York* (York). Interleaved copy in York Central Library containing ms. additions by Drake.

Duckham, B.F. (1967) *The Yorkshire Ouse* (Newton Abbot).

Dunn, C.J. (1976) 'Ring ditches in the Derwent valley', *Rep. Yorkshire Philosoph. Soc. for 1975,* 60.

Elgee, F. and H.W. (1933) *The Archaeology of Yorkshire* (London).

Faull, M.L. (1974) 'Roman and Anglian settlement patterns in Yorkshire', *Northern History,* ix, 1.

Fox, C. (1958) *Pattern and Purpose* (Cardiff).

Frere, S.S. (1961) 'Civitas: a Myth', *Antiquity* xxxv, 29.

Frere, S.S. (1974) *Britannia* (2nd. ed. London).

Goodall, I.H. (1969) *The Roman villas of East Yorkshire,* unpublished dissertation.

Goodall, I.H. (1972) 'Industrial evidence from the villa at Langton, East Yorkshire', *Yorkshire Archaeol. J.* xliv, 32.

Harris, A. (1961) *The rural landscape of the East Riding of Yorkshire, 1700-1850* (Oxford).

Hartley, B.R. (1971) 'Roman York and the northern military command to the third century A.D.', *in* Butler, *1971,* 55.

Hawkes, S.C. and Dunning, G.C. (1961) 'Soldiers and settlers in Britain, fourth to fifth centuries', *Medieval Archaeol.* v, 1.

Hayes, R.H. (1958) 'Romano-British dwelling sites in north and east Yorkshire', *Trans. Scarborough and District Archaeol. Soc.* i, 26.

Hayes, R.H. and Rutter, J.G. (1964) *Wade's Causeway,* Res. Rep. Scarborough and District Archaeol. Soc., no. 4.

Hayes, R.H. and Whitley, E. (1950) *The Roman pottery kiln at Norton, East Yorkshire,* Roman Malton and District Rep. no. 7. (Leeds).

Haynes, J. (1744) *An accurate survey of ... Roman Remains in the Wolds of Yorkshire,* engraved by G. Vertue (London).

Hicks, J.D. and Wilson J.A. (1975) 'The Romano-British kilns at Hasholme, East Riding', *East Riding Archaeol.* ii, 49.

Hornsby, W. and Stanton, R. (1912) 'The Roman fort at Huntcliff, near Saltburn', *J. Roman Stud.* ii, 215.

Hornsby, W. and Laverick, J.D. (1932) 'The Roman signal station at Goldsborough near Whitby', *Archaeol. J.* lxxxix, 203.

Hull, M.R. (1932) 'The pottery from the Roman signal-stations on the Yorkshire coast', *Archaeol. J.* lxxxix, 220.

Jackson, K. (1948) 'On some Romano-British Place-names', *J. Roman Stud.* xxxviii, 57.

Jackson, K. (1970) 'Romano-British names in the Antonine Itinerary', *in* Rivet *1970*, 68.

Jones, M.J. (1975) *Roman Fort-defences to A.D. 117*, British Arch. Reps., no. 21 (Oxford).

King, E.M. and Moore, M. (1975) 'The Romano-British settlement at Crambe, North Yorkshire', *Rep. Yorkshire Philosoph. Soc. for 1974*, 64.

Liversidge, J., Smith, D.J. and Stead, I.M. (1973) 'Brantingham Roman Villa: Discoveries in 1962', *Britannia* iv, 84.

Lloyd, G.D. (1968) 'A Roman pottery kiln in the parish of Lockington', *East Riding Archaeol.* i, 28.

McInnes, I.J. (1968) 'The excavation of a Bronze Age cemetery at Catfoss, East Yorkshire', *East Riding Archaeol.* i, 1.

Margary, I.D. (1967) *Roman Roads in Britain* (2nd. ed. London).

Marshall, W. (1788) *The Rural Economy of Yorkshire* (London).

Mellor, E. (1956) *Harpham Roman Villa*, unpublished typescript.

Mellor, E. (1952) 'The Harpham Villa', *Yorkshire Archaeol. J.* xxxviii, 117.

Mitchelson, N. (1964) 'Roman Malton: the civilian settlement, excavations in Orchard Field, 1949-52', *Yorkshire Archaeol. J.*, xli, 209.

Moore, J.W. (1965) 'An Anglo-Saxon settlement at Wykeham, North Yorkshire', *Yorkshire Archaeol. J.* xli, 403.

Morris, J. (1966) 'Dark Ages dates', *in* Jarrett, M.G. and Dobson, B. (eds.), *Britain and Rome* (Kendal).

Morris, J. (1973) *The Age of Arthur* (London).

Mortimer, R. (1886) *A Restoration of the Ancient British Entrenchments and Tumuli also the surface geology and modern enclosure of Fimber in the Yorkshire Wolds* (Fimber, York).

Mortimer, J.R. (1905) *Forty Years Researches in British and Saxon Burial Mounds of East Yorkshire* (London).

Myres, J.N.L. (1969) *Anglo-Saxon pottery and the settlement of England* (Oxford).

Myres, J.N.L. and Southern, W.H. (1973) *The Anglo-Saxon cremation cemetery at Sancton, East Yorkshire*, Hull Museum Publication no. 218.

Norman, A.F. (1961) *The Romans in East Yorkshire*, East Yorkshire Local History Series, no. 12.

Piggott, S. (1958) 'Native economies and the Roman Occupation of North Britain', *in* Richmond *1958*.

Pocock, M. (1971) 'A buckle plate and the Anglo-Saxon brooches from Catterick', *Yorkshire Archaeol. J.* xliii, 187-8.

Radley, J. and Simms, C. (1970) *Yorkshire Flooding – Some effects on Man and Nature* (York).

Ramm, H.G. (1955) 'A Romano-British kiln, and the Roman road at Stamford Bridge', *Yorkshire Archaeol. J.* xxxviii, 552.

Ramm, H.G. (1966) 'The Derwent crossing at Stamford Bridge', *Yorkshire Archaeol. J.* xli, 587.

Ramm, H.G. (1971) 'The end of Roman York', *in* Butler *1971*, 179.

Ramm, H.G. (1972) 'Foreword', *in* Reader *1972*, ix.

Ramm, H.G. (1976a) 'Roman Roads west of Tadcaster', *York Historian* i, 3.

Ramm, H.G. (1976b) 'Excavations on the site of St. Mary's Church, Bishophill Senior', *Yorkshire Archaeol. J.* xlviii, 35.

Ramm, H.G., McDowall, R.W. and Mercer, E. (1970) *Shielings and Bastles* (London).

RCHM (1962), *An Inventory of the Historical Monuments in the City of York, i, Eburacum, Roman York* (London).

Reader, E.M. (1972) *Broomfleet and Faxfleet, two townships through two thousand years* (York).

Richmond, I.A. (1932) Review of Corder and Kirk *1932*, *J. Roman Stud.* xxii, 255.

Richmond, I.A. (1933) 'The four Roman camps at Cawthorn, in the North Riding of Yorkshire', *Archaeol. J.* lxxxix, 17.

Richmond, I.A. (1947) 'The four coloniae of Roman Britain', *Archaeol. J.* ciii, 37.

Richmond, I.A. (1954a) 'Queen Cartimandua', *J. Roman Stud.* xliv, 43.

Richmond, I.A. (1954b) 'Geography of Brigantia', *in* Wheeler *1954*, 61.

Richmond, I.A. (1955) *Roman Britain* (Harmondsworth).

Richmond, I.A. (ed.) (1958) *Roman and Native in North Britain* (London).

Richmond, I.A. (1966) 'Industry in Roman Britain', *in* Wacher *1966*, 76.

Richmond, I.A. and Crawford, O.G.S. (1949) 'The British section of the Ravenna Cosmosgraphy', *Archaeologia* xclii, 1.

Riley, D.N. (1973) 'Aerial reconnaisance of the West Riding magnesian limestone country', *Yorkshire Archaeol. J.* xlv, 210.

Riley, D.N. (1974) 'Brief report on recent archaeological flying', *Yorks. Archaeol. J.* xlvi, 183.

Riley, D.N. (1975) 'Recent archaeological reconnaisance from the air', *Yorks. Archaeol. J.* xlvii, 11.

Rivet, A.L.F. (1958) *Town and Country in Roman Britain* (London).

Rivet, A.L.F. (ed.) (1969) *The Roman Villa in Britain* (London).

Rivet, A.L.F. (1970) 'The British section of the Antonine Itinerary', *J. Roman Stud.* i, 34.

Rodwell, W. (1975) 'Milestones, civic territories and the Antonine Itinerary', *Britannia* vi, 76.

Rutter, J.G. and Duke, G. (1958) *Excavations at Crossgates near Scarborough 1947-56*, Res. Rep. Scarborough and District Archaeol. Soc. no. 1.

Rowntree, A. (ed.) (1931) *The History of Scarborough* (London).

Sheppard, J.A. (1966) *The Draining of the Marshlands of South Holderness and the Vale of York*, East Yorkshire Local History Series, no. 20 (York).

Sheppard, T. (1905) *Roman villa at Harpham*, Hull Museum Publication, no. 23.

Sheppard, T. (1913) 'East Yorkshire History in plan and chart', *Trans. East Riding Antiq. Soc.* xix, 40.

Sheppard, T. (1938) 'Excavations at Eastburn, East Yorkshire', *Yorkshire Archaeol. J.* xxxiv, 35.

Simpson, G. (1973) 'Roman Manchester and Templeborough: The forts and dates reviewed', *in* Hawkes, C.F.C. and S.C. (eds.) *Greeks, Celts, and Romans*, 69.

Smith, D.J. (1969) 'The mosaic pavements', *in* Rivet *1969*, 71.

Smith, D.J. (1976) *The Roman mosaics from Rudston, Brantingham and Horkstow* (Hull)

Smith, R.A. (1927) 'Pre-Roman remains at Scarborough', *Archaeologia* lxxvii, 179.

Smythe, J.A. (1940) 'Roman pigs of lead from Brough', *Trans. Newcomen Soc.*, xx, 139.

Stead, I.M. (1961) 'A distinctive form of La Tène barrow in Eastern Yorkshire and on the continent', *Antiq. J.* xli, 44.

Stead, I.M. (1965) *The La Tene cultures of Eastern Yorkshire* (York).

Stead, I.M. (1968), 'An Iron Age hill fort at Grimthorpe, Yorkshire, England', *Proc. Prehist. Soc.* xxxiv, 148.

Stead, I.M. (1971a) Yorkshire before the Romans: some recent discoveries', *in* Butler *1971*, 21.

Stead, I.M. (1971b) 'Beadlam Roman villa: an interim report', *Yorkshire Archaeol. J.* xliii, 178.

Stead, I.M. (1977) *Winterton Roman villa and other Roman sites in North Lincolnshire*, Dept. of Environment, Res. Rep. no. 9.

Swanton, J.M. (1967) 'An early Alamannic brooch from Yorkshire', *Antiq. J.* xlvii, 43.

Todd, M. (1973) *The Coritani* (London).

Varley, W.J. (1968) 'Barmston and the Holderness Crannogs', *East Riding Archaeol.* i, 12.

Wacher, J.S. (ed.) (1966) *Civitas Capitals of Roman Britain* (Leicester).

Wacher, J.S. (1969) *Excavations at Brough on Humber, 1958-61*, Res. Rep. Soc. Antiq. London, no. 25.

Wacher, J.S. (1971) 'Yorkshire towns in the fourth century', *in* Butler *1971*, 165.

Wacher, J.S. (1974) *The Towns of Roman Britain* (London).

Wainwright, G.J. and Longworth, I.H. (1969) 'The excavation of a group of round barrows on Ampleforth Moor, Yorkshire', *Yorkshire Archaeol. J.* xlii, 283.

Webster, G. (1969) 'The future of villa studies', *in* Rivet *1969*, 246.

Wenham, L.P. (1960) 'Seven archaeological discoveries in Yorkshire', *Yorkshire Archaeol. J.* xl, 298.

Wenham, L.P. (1967) 'Five archaeological discoveries in Yorkshire', *Rep. Yorkshire Philosophical Soc. for 1966*, 23.

Wenham, L.P. (1968), *The Romano-British cemetery at Trentholme Drive, York*, Ministry of Public Buildings and Works, Res. Rep. no. 5 (London).

Wenham, L.P. (1971) 'The beginnings of Roman York,' *in* Butler *1971*, 45.

Wenham, L.P. (1974) *Derventio (Malton): Roman fort and civil settlement* (Huddersfield).

Wheeler, R.E.M. (1931) 'Prehistoric Scarborough', *in* Rowntree *1931*, 9.

Wheeler, R.E.M. (1954) *The Stanwick Fortifications*, Res. Rep. Soc. Ant. London, no. 17.

Woodward, A.M. (1934) 'The Roman villa at Rudston: interim excavation report', *Yorkshire Archaeol. J.* xxxi, 366.

Woodward, A.M. (1935) 'The Roman villa at Rudston: second interim report', *Yorkshire Archaeol. J.* xxxii, 214.

Woodward, A.M. and Steer K.A. (1936) 'The Roman villa at Rudston: third interim report', *Yorkshire Archaeol. J.* xxxiii, 81.

Index